"*A Friend Sails in on a Poem* is a rare and beautiful book: a double portrait of a long-lasting friendship, beginning with the way that poetry brought Molly Peacock and Phillis Levin together, and then tracing their lives backwards and forwards through poems and remembrances before arriving in our post pandemic world. I had the good fortune of being Phillis's student and then assistant and then friend, so of course, I've also had the good fortune of knowing Molly. In revisiting these stories and poems, I realize how many of my own literary relationships have been modeled on the alchemical mix of intellectual rigor and personal tenderness that has structured their friendship. The paradoxical truth of poetry is that poems are both intimate and public: the best parts of ourselves stripped bare, and then sent into the world. Reading this book, I understand that truth in a new way."
— Jason Schneiderman, author of *Hold Me Tight*

"A poem's structure can hold, in rhythms, rules, and careful architecture, the intensities of a poet's sensitive appreciation of the world. Molly Peacock's tribute to her nearly half-century friendship with fellow poet Phillis Levin suggests that rhythms and structures also gently hold the passion and intensity of a deeply creative and aesthetically fulfilling bond between two women. When the demands of day-to-day life make it almost impossible to stay in touch with raw awareness, a poet needs to find a way to protect her ability to stay open to relationship with the wondrous universe. And through regular get-togethers, meal rituals and gentle rules for offering each other support, Molly and Phllis find a special rhythm that sustains them. Their friendship pulses, like a line's metre, through decades of their lives, offering life-blood and protection to two poets' ardent hearts."
— Sonnet L'Abbe, author of *Sonnet's Shakespeare*

"Whatever the subject, rich music follows the tap of Molly Peacock's baton."
— *Washington Post*

"Ms. Peacock uses rhyme and meter as a way to cut reality into sizeable chunks, the sense of the poem spilling from line to line, breathlessly."
— *The New York Times Book Review*

"When John Stuart Mill wrote "eloquence is heard, but poetry is overheard," he could have been describing one of the bittersweet pleasures of Molly Peacock's poems."
— *O, the Oprah Magazine*

"Peacock's ethos is less about acclaiming the ordinary than examining human relationships in all their permutations and depth. With the exquisite technical prowess she brings to bear, that is anything but ordinary."
— *The Times Literary Supplement*

"Peacock's orderly grace can seem paradoxical when she's describing intense, chaotic emotions. But that lyrical craft is exactly what makes her poems resonate."
— *Toronto Star*

"With Peacock, the human body heals two by two."
— *Poetry*

"Peacock has many talents, not the least of which is her voice, characterized by engaging honesty and self-deprecating humor. She comes across as that fellow passenger on an airplane to whom you have suddenly and quite naturally confessed your story (and learned hers)."
— *The Hudson Review*

A FRIEND SAILS IN ON A POEM

A Friend Sails in on a Poem

With an Afterword
by Phillis Levin

Molly Peacock

Palimpsest Press
1171 Eastlawn Ave.
Windsor, Ontario, N8S 3J1
www.palimpsestpress.ca

Printed and bound in Canada
Cover design and book typography by Ellie Hastings
Series Editor Jim Johnstone
Edited by Jason Guriel
Copyedited by Ashley Van Elswyk

Palimpsest Press would like to thank the Canada Council for the
Arts and the Ontario Arts Council for their support of our publishing program. We also acknowledge the assistance of the Government
of Ontario through the Ontario Book Publishing Tax Credit.

LIBRARY AND ARCHIVES CANADA CATALOGUING IN PUBLICATION

TITLE: A friend sails in on a poem / Molly Peacock.
NAMES: Peacock, Molly, 1947- author.
IDENTIFIERS: Canadiana (print) 20220280355
                        Canadiana (ebook) 20220280363

ISBN 9781990293306 (SOFTCOVER)
ISBN 9781990293313 (EPUB)
ISBN 9781990293320 (PDF)
SUBJECTS: LCSH: POETICS. | LCSH: FRIENDSHIP. | LCGFT: ESSAYS.
CLASSIFICATION: LCC PS3566.E15 F75 2022 | DDC C814/.54—DC23

For all those friends who make art together

"Friends are our families now"

AUTHOR'S NOTE

A Friend Sails in on a Poem is a memoir of an aesthetic friendship. The intimacy of the conversations, the diary entries, and even the tables (from seminar to kitchen to restaurant tables) where our story evolved, all evoke realms personal in nature. Though the poet Phillis Levin and I have written poems touching on everything from nuclear war to ecological disasters, I have stayed with work that speaks to me of our private lives, grateful to my friend who read, commented on, and tolerated every word I wrote.

Molly Peacock, Toronto

TABLE OF CONTENTS

Chapter One:
A Friend Sails in on a Poem

1.

It is lost on neither of us that inside *friendship* the word "ship" sails beside the word "friend." Phillis Levin and I, two poets, have played with words since learning to speak—and we delight in discovering that a living noun like *friend* is companion to a living suffix like *ship* (also a noun). We love our art—it has probably saved our lives—and through our poems we have almost written our relationship with one another. For forty-six years we've each read almost every line the other has composed. *Friend*, both of us know very well, derives from *Freund*, or love.

How have we lasted almost half a century?

We are continents apart aesthetically. We are tiers apart in origins and class. You could not tell we were friends by our hair. (One's is luxurious, pre-Raphaelite, long, and still brunette; the other's is straight, thin, gray-blonde, and bobbed.) Yet an Anglo-Saxon riddle might describe both of our souls. Here's one, just to keep the sailing metaphor going, a translation of mine:

Ship's Figurehead

I was a girl,   a gray queen,
and a man, solo,   all in a single hour.
I flew with the birds   swam in the seas
dove under waves   died with the fishes
and stepped out on earth   —alive, all in a single soul.[1]

There is a weird way, in our conversations about poetry, that we share a single soul. But let's not get too spiritual about it. Basically, what we share is food (we have been eating meals while talking poetry for nearly five decades) as well as thoughts about how words animate feelings. A beet salad or a lemon poppyseed pancake enhances our arcane, secret sort of refuge for the adults we are, and the children we were.

We were white girls, in the Anglo-Saxon binary sense, and simultaneously queens, in the Anglo-Saxon teacher-woman-leader sense, and we were men, in the think-and-act-like-a-man sense of how we were educated, and we transformed ourselves: the daughter of a comfortable middle-class Jewish family in Paterson, New Jersey—that's Phillis. A Christian working-class girl with Canadian settler roots from Tonawanda, New York—that's me. We flew through our lives like birds (and crashed into windows, too), we swam in the seas that transported us from desperate fear, and dove under the waves in attempt after attempt to make our lives; we came out onto earth as grown humans, alive in the poems we made and witnessed each other making.

2.

In our decades together, other relationships have slipped and slid away. Sometimes, one of us has lived alone, without a primary love relationship; sometimes, the other has. We both have reveled in the deep pleasure of profoundly satisfying marriages, though I live solo now, since my husband of twenty-eight years, the James Joyce scholar Michael Groden, died. At different times, Phillis and I have moved into one another's somewhat abandoned spaces, like hermit crabs, darting to temporary homes. In the 1990s, Phillis once spent weekends in the tiny East 71st Street New York studio apartment I no longer lived in but used as a writing space. In 2008, I spent almost a year subletting her small one-bedroom Manhattan co-op on West 110th Street. Phillis only used it intermittently then. She kept it for a few years after marrying cardiothoracic anesthesiologist Dr. Jack Shanewise.

One day during that time, I was walking along Broadway when I saw, in the window of a little stationery store, some file folders with a Navy blue and brown geometric print. I knew Phillis would love them. I bought them but didn't have a chance to wrap them up. In a hurry, I slipped them on a shelf behind the brown leather chair I had repositioned in her living room.

Weeks before, when I moved in, I had felt perfectly free to charge in and rearrange all of Phillis's furniture—including some files! How many other friends would tolerate your reshuffling of their rug, couch, chairs, and objects? Yet, Phillis was thrilled. An enthusiast to the bottom of her soul, she hopped up and down like a seven-year-old, flapping her arms. *Look what you did for the coffee table!* It was as if she had witnessed a miracle. All I had done was put a throw rug in front of the blue couch and anchor both with a coffee table that had been sitting forlornly in a corner after a guest had shifted it there to open the sofa bed. I brought nothing new to this room but a waterglass full of flowers and a cereal bowl full of tangerines. But like a narrative poem whose stanzas have been re-sequenced, the room had begun to make sense. It was on its way to becoming warm, comforting, and whole.

Phillis freely admits that she tends to be passive about her environments, adapting to, rather than changing them. She gives the impression that she has no sense of how to arrange a room—though she certainly knows how to arrange a stanza with great beauty. (*Stanza* is Italian for *room*; you can think of the stanzas as rooms in the little apartments of poems.) I am in awe of Phillis's revision process, but I attribute her spatial mystification to my friend's rarely being allowed as a child to have freedom of movement. She was never permitted to cross the street by herself. The doors and windows of her house were locked. Her grandmother, with whom she and her brother and parents lived, kept the keys in her pocket and even, to demonstrate her adult power, sometimes waved them tantalizingly in front of her granddaughter's face. "If someone is imprisoned," Phillis reminded me in a recent conversation, "they discover their inner world."

At a certain age, far beyond the point where most children learn to grip a banister and start to climb down steps, Phillis stood hesitating at the top of a flight of stairs. Her grandmother decided it was time to teach her. So, Phillis learned from an arthritic septuagenarian how to pick her way down, placing her feet sideways, one by one, in the manner of an ancient lady whose ankles no longer worked. And she still descends steep steps sideways.

Though born seven years apart, and growing up with entirely different senses of how to interact with space, we connected in what we loved at similar ages. In 1954, while Phillis was a squalling infant in her mother's arms in Paterson, my mother was escorting me, age seven, to a chock-a-block hardware emporium in north Buffalo. (In 1961, when Phillis was seven, she would adore being taken by her father on his errands to another such wondrous hardware store.) I was to choose a color for the bedroom that I shared with my little sister. Among the screwdrivers and pliers and brushes and copper tubing of this store, I discovered that there were inch-square paint chips from which a person somehow was to extrapolate what a whole room would look like. My mother let me take some home, where I spent hours deciding between Seafoam Green and Lavender for the bedroom walls. My dilemma was between a color and the romantic name of another color. I wanted a purple room, but lavender was a word I already knew. I teetered on the green because of the adjective seafoam. A color comprised of two words! It would invite the sea and its foam to drench the bedroom. But the reality of seafoam was merely pale green, and, really, I wanted purple.

The paint chips offered a contradictory wonder: the color and the name of the color. In the end I forsook the romance of the name on one chip for the visual fact of the other. But it was so wrenching I recall the choice sixty-seven years later in an odd kind of almost physically painful psychic disjunct: Why couldn't the name match the color? Isn't the name the thing?? This was a needle of agony for me, a nascent poet who didn't know it. Three years later I knew it, though, and, at ten, wrote my first verse. And twenty-two years later, I would meet another young person who would relate exactly to that experience. A friend would sail in on a poem.

There was Phillis at the end of a seminar table in Gilman Hall at the Johns Hopkins University Writing Seminars; Phillis, who had had a talismanic childhood experience with a Pink Pearl pencil eraser almost the size of a paint chip.

Phillis would erase and save the rubber shavings to make nest material for the little boxes she hoarded. (I think they must have been jewelry boxes.) She touched the rubber shreds as if they were skin. Then, she put cherished things in their nests: a newspaper clipping all folded up, or a marble she loved named Allie. She still has Allie, an opaque white aggie with umber swirls, by the way. Allie, whose name is short for Alligator, was with her in Baltimore. (Phillis thought "alligator" was a color, the shade of the skin of the stuffed reptile her grandmother brought back from Florida.)

"I didn't want to play with dolls," Phillis expostulated one day when we were waiting for our carrot ginger soup to cool. (Me either.) "I created very elaborate scenarios with my pet marble on a small scale."

BOX IN EDEN
by Phillis Levin

Pink Pearl eraser
rubbing white paper,
diminishing into
a little hill, more

and more so the box
can fill: little container
a perfect promise,
ready to hold the feel

of skin, ready to nestle
a fingernail clipping,
a button, a marble,
a tooth or a pin.

Pink Pearl collecting,
sifted, sifting:
embers of kindness,
a bower of crumbs.

Here resides
whatever in itself
by itself
is enough

to touch, eyes closed,
not to covet or possess,
only to caress —
and where is it now,

my secret compartment,
humble casket,
barrow of being,
storehouse of

unsayable softness
unclaimed, asleep
at the bottom
of what drawer?

Both Phillis's eraser and my paint swatch vibrated in our memories the way rectangular phones now vibrate in our pockets. They represented finely discriminated long-ago moments. Remembered in exquisite detail. Gems. Far, far from the everyday worlds inhabited by girls who, back then, faced a slim list of occupations. But we would not be nurses, teachers, homemakers, waitresses, secretaries, or assistant forest rangers. We would be poets.

After my parents painted my room lavender, it was transformed! One activity had changed a whole entity. The same yellow toy box that my father designed and constructed now glowed; the white chenille bedspreads that my mother bleached now softened, all because a color that encased the entire structure was newly fixed. The room was now whole. And this applies to the wholeness of a poem, too. A poem is an assemblage of many parts, and all the parts can change and come into order with a single large structural decision. Hewing to the idea of the whole prevents me from overdetermining certain details that I can't quite get right. I simply must leave the slips and flaws there—and eventually my mistakes, though still annoying me, find their own blemished place in the overall scheme—whether it's a sonnet, a villanelle, or a galloping narrative with a refrain.

But Phillis perceives entirely differently from me.

After I hid the files on the bookshelf behind the brown leather chair, the doorman announced her. When she walked in, she spied, from 12 feet away, a half-inch corner of one of the folders slipping out from its hiding place.

"What's that?" she asked.

Damn it, it was the Levin Eagle Eye! Somehow, she riveted on that tiniest of tiny details. I think this predilection, this skill, accounts for the surface of her poems. Phillis is a champ at minute perception. The slight jarring of vocabulary or rhythm inside one of her poems can drive her into revisions meticulously labeled A to K, or beyond, from L to R, and even on occasion to Z. (I have seen the revisions go to the next alphabet of double letters; I think JJ may be the furthest a vocabulary change went.) Just short of dumbfounded stupefaction, I observe her process. For decades I have watched her poems slowly, slowly inch themselves out of the page (oh yes, we are committed to paper) in draft after draft. It's like watching time-lapse tendrils climbing up a fence.

I have multiple drafts, too, but rarely as many. Such a concentrated process would beat a poem of mine into unconsciousness. I'd have to wheel it into a prosody emergency room. But I think of Phillis as subscribing to James McNeill Whistler's premise that paint should be applied "as breath on glass."[2] She builds a tonal surface through precise vocabulary almost the way a painter conjures an atmosphere through evenness of brushstrokes. That's why the half-inch square of a blue and brown pattern on a folder hidden in a bookcase behind a chair in a room can become strangely, deeply meaningful.

"What's that?"

"It's a present for you. I didn't have a chance to wrap it."

"Quick-eyed," as George Herbert, the seventeenth-century mystic poet would say, Phillis saw that jot of a geometric design. It seemed she didn't think to move the coffee table in front of the couch. Inside this spatial contradiction—and the delight, the ecstatic delight at the half-inch square of pattern—somehow, somewhere, forms the seed of a poem for Phillis. It is a mystery to me. A forty-six-year friendship mystery.

The sources of other people's creativity mystify me, too. When I was young, I used to extrapolate from my own creative process, thinking that everyone's method was like mine, and teaching like that, as well. But truly examining how another person gets to the writing and finishing of a poem has chastened me into modesty about how art comes to be in the world. Now, the only thing I can say for certain is: *Isn't it amazing? Something has been made out of nothing.*

3.

For longer than I've known Phillis, I've been acquainted with the work of the French phenomenologist Gaston Bachelard, author of *The Poetics of Space*. Bachelard was obsessed with architectural structures, like houses and rooms. Me, too, obviously. There was even a time when I wrote the occasional article for *House & Garden* magazine. It's not only the rectangles of rooms that repeat stanza structures, but other architectural rectangles, like window frames, that can set up a new sense of psychic space.

The opening poem in *Temples and Fields*, the first book Phillis put out to the world, is "Something About Windows." In it, she watches a couple eating a meal at the next table in a restaurant. "What to make of conversations flickering," Phillis writes, as the "She" in the poem "Extols the intricate layers a salad/ Can hide to entice and surprise." Then, some lines later, Levin (and I'm going to call Phillis by her last name here, because the work I am considering is that of Levin, crisp on the page) turns toward the idea of a window and writes: "feeling/ Diffuses through this sheet glass/ Where forgetfulness and memory kiss/ Without falling for each other." Windows will come into the poem in the next line: "Yet there is something about windows."

The photographer Diane Arbus's brother, Howard Nemerov, wrote a poem about these apertures that I've loved since I was secretly deciding at nineteen (well, was it a decision or a calling?) to be a poet, if a girl from blue-collar Buffalo (attending a state university in an era of anthologies that featured white male poets largely from Harvard) could call herself such a thing. Nemerov titled his poem, "Storm Windows," an item so rare now that his poem seems almost historical. He describes the storm windows lying on the grass because it has begun to rain, driving the householders inside before their jobs can be completed. He sees "The ripple and splash of rain on the blurred glass" and the window seems to speak: "it briefly said, as I walked by/ Something I should have liked to say to you,/ Something…" but we never learn what.

Levin incorporates that "Something" into her title, and then unfolds it. "Yet there is something about windows// That makes me want to tell/ The story of my past."

Those rectangles of glass offer a way into both poets' lives. In each poem, the rain rushes across the pane (*pain?*). The young poet Levin writes of herself still younger, as a child, "How I traced the life of a raindrop/ As it raced to the sill." And she "can't wait" to begin her adult life, till childhood "was over,"

> …till the flat
> Four-cornered room of childhood
> Ended, as the globe came into sight
> And my hand extended.

Phillis Levin's youthful poem is far more optimistic than Howard Nemerov's. It's the lead poem in the debut volume of a poet who would go on to write many more, to inhabit the globe, to extend her hand to experience. But it also has a little of the loneliness of Nemerov, who wrote "of memories/ And missed desires" along with his memorable line in parentheses "(Unspeakable, the distance in the mind!)."[3]

So, as friends, we were enamored of rectangles. They were apertures into the lives we sought to understand by describing them with sound, imagery, and thoughts all recombined into lines and stanzas. Our poems, so different, were both made of the raw material of the incomprehensibilities of our lives. We gave them sound systems, highlighting a single image or two, and mined for syntax that would yield some meaning. "The Lawns of June," the last poem in my first book, *And Live Apart,* was chock full of rectangles (*tangles?*).

> The lawns of June, flush with the walks and white
> driveways of town, grow and are mown. The grid
> of lawn after lawn, then drive after drive,
> the 90-degree angles of walks, roads
> stripped and then tarred flush with the curbs...

The young Molly Peacock saw the grids as "what any troubled mind or body/ would order" to calm confusion. The poem ends the brightly lit suburban day with evening, and the soothing murmur of a couple talking in bed. She doesn't say it, but those are her parents, usually so distraught, so worried about money, so unable to communicate, so full of frustration and anger toward one another, that for her to hear them on occasion calmly speaking back and forth, was a sudden palliation. It put everything in order, just like those lawns. She attached that imagery to a painter whose work she still loves, Richard Diebenkorn. He used rectangular shapes to display the suburban landscape in paintings she saw again and again at the Albright-Knox Art Gallery in Buffalo. (Later, it turned out that Levin loved Diebenkorn, too.)

Rectangular shapes repeat stanza structures. Phillis's poem has seven stanzas. It is orderly and elegant as it unfolds. Mine has one. Everything crushed into one space? Hmmmm…a single stanza as a landscape. A portrait of my mind then.

SOMETHING ABOUT WINDOWS
by Phillis Levin

In the distance are the horses,
In the distance is the noon.
The moon is a long way off, a long time.
When did space separate
From the meticulous counting down
Of beginning leaf and scattered petal?

Pauses, sirens, dust, pollen, light.
It is spring, but none before like this.
What to make of conversations flickering,
Playing in and out of meaning
With an ease that bears resemblance
To the congenial balance of sun and shade.

She, who sits at the table next,
Extols the intricate layers a salad
Can hide to entice and surprise,
Subtle and cool as a banker's eyes.
He chooses from the menu without wonder;
No hurry, the day is far from over.

But what was that green change
Crossing his retina?
Just a woman's back, covered
In mint—her silk shirt's fluctuation
As she strides past kids on bicycles,
Graphic in their perfection.

Freed from longing
For my face in another, feeling
Diffuses through this sheet of glass,
Where forgetfulness and memory kiss
Without falling for each other.
Yet there is something about windows

That makes me want to tell
The story of my past:
How I traced the life of a raindrop
As it raced to the sill,
How a wish split the wishbone
And the truth divided.

The sky was once suspended
By silver chords of sound.
But I couldn't wait
Till it was over, till the flat
Four-cornered room of childhood
Ended, as the globe came into sight
And my hand extended.

THE LAWNS OF JUNE
by Molly Peacock

The lawns of June, flush with the walks and white
driveways of town, grow and are mown. The grid
of lawn after lawn, then drive after drive,
the 90-degree angles of walks, roads
stripped and then tarred flush with the curbs, all these,
smooth, regular as the rules on a fresh
white card pulled from the box of a new game,
or fresh and regular as the game board
itself, the squares prime for our leaping plays,
are what any troubled mind or body
would order: such as, from here to the drug
store is forty-seven lawns, one hundred-
six lawns from here to the veterinary.
It feels good to count in these ways. And smooth,
the sidewalks and streets are very smooth.
An octagonal sign says Stop. Two lines
mean School. The lawns are thick chartreuse gouache,
roads black as silk, straight and fine as surgical
silk, the walks are bandage white. How smooth and
fast the wheels of cars and bikes and skates go,
their yearning unyielding. These geometries
are love's tired proofs: the badinage of wheel
and road and walk and lawn and drive and curb
and sign and line all flush, flushed with a soft
raillery of values laying the grids
we make with one another, a couple
talking in bed, a water glass near
the Bible, a child's torn bear in his arm.

Chapter Two:
Makers of our Lives

1.

To be the makers, the *scops* of our lives. *Scop*, or poet, doesn't mean "singer" in Anglo-Saxon; it means "maker." That's what both Phillis and I wanted when the seed of our friendship blew into Baltimore in the fall of 1976 and rooted at the Writing Seminars at Johns Hopkins University. At the opposite end of the seminar table sat a twenty-two-year-old Phillis in a plaid flannel shirt. At my end, I was newly divorced, twenty-nine-years old, and poured into a pair of straight leg linen pants so tight they pulled at the seams a little bit like the sonnets I was teaching myself to write. (Those sonnets always seemed to go slightly past that 14th line.) We were fresh and excited— and chosen from among many applicants, for there were only fourteen handpicked members of the class. We sat at the table with two brilliant American poets who would become lifelong friends, Rachel Hadas and Thomas Sleigh, and another shining talent who later became a novelist, Lisa Zeidner.

Capping the uniform of plaid shirt and jeans, a single strand of graduated pearls rested on Phillis's collarbone.

(Phillis corrects me about those pearls. She acquired them much later. But she talked so often about a pearl necklace, withheld by her family, that my memory gives them to her just when she wanted them.) An onyx ring with a tiny inlaid bird rested on her large, long hand.[4] She had just graduated from Sarah Lawrence College where she had determined to become a psychologist. Though she knew she was destined to become a poet, Hopkins was a detour on the way to a PhD in psychology. But for me, Hopkins was a direct station on the path to my calling.

Seven years before, I had graduated from the State University of New York at Binghamton, then married, worked at the university, started to publish poems, and been accepted at MacDowell for an artists residency. *Why do you want to go to graduate school???* The other young prize-winning poets at the MacDowell dinner table—Peter Klappert, Hugh Seidman, Carol Muske, and Philip Schultz—would inevitably ask. "Because I don't know anything," I said. I felt I needed to know everything about prosodic technique, the things that John Keats knew, that Milton knew, that Chaucer understood. Even though I would have described myself as a feminist, the poets I felt I should be able to emulate were all white, all male. If I absorbed their techniques and used them, I'd be taken seriously.

But then I discovered Marianne Moore, Gabriela Mistral, Elizabeth Bishop, Gwendolyn Brooks, Gertrude Stein, Elinor Wylie. I went back to Li Ch'ing Chao. Shiki. Issa. I sat in the verbal whirlpool of Jerome Rothenberg's anthology, *Technicians of the Sacred*. It was my first exposure to Anishinabe poetry. Poems from the earliest centuries came hurtling at me.

A balky forest-green Audi was among the spoils from my divorce. Sometimes I gave Phillis rides downtown or to the Baltimore Museum of Art where the Cone collection of

Henri Matisse paintings hung. It was a separate world, with a more intense color wheel than the real life of macadam and brick, like the palette of Henri's intense Fauvist paintings. Almost instantly we loved talking about poetry together—and childhood. Phillis enthused about her pre-verbal perceptions. I effused about my childhood observations. We felt the sharpness of our earliest discernments, the clean, singular feelings of thrill or abandonment or fear that formed our ways of going through the world and shaped our approaches to poetry. If only I could express what I saw so vividly in my head, crystalline, sometimes terrifying memories of people, light, animals, landscape. Phillis would become absorbed in the objects of childhood, often in locked cabinets.

Phillis seemed all intellect. She seemed to float through air, as if she were made of air. "I used to be ethereal," reads the first line of her poem, "Definition," in her second book, *The Afterimage*.

> I used to be ethereal:
> It was my natural state
> To be detached, removed, indifferent,
> Not to others but to myself.

I instantly attached to her quick associations—how smart she was!

In my natural state I felt all body. When I wasn't eating and writing in my nightgown, I was having sex with my new boyfriend. My influences were the confessional poets. I longed to write "What really happened," as Elizabeth Hardwick advised Robert Lowell. Yet, I felt if I actually *did* say what happened, to try to make poetry out of the ordeals of my family, it wouldn't really be poetry at all—just what our professors called "mere self-expression."

Deep inside the pink-and-white box of a suburban house,

post-World War II trauma, violence, and alcohol: the heated sexual charge of a hurt, ham-fisted veteran. The helpless, drained face of his wife. Two little girls at their legs. The vet in his T-shirt prods the wife backwards. Cellar door open. Monster-mouth yawning. Instead of a tongue, steep stairs down to the coal bin. He pushes toward her, as she screams while the little girls sneak down through their tangle of adult legs to push back up.

How was I to take my father and mother and the never spoken of scenes that would later be called abuse and make art of them? The house, a rectangle; the cellar door, a rectangle; the stairs, a long rectangle; the poem, a rectangle, the stanzas descending like stairs.

2.

Though Phillis was absorbed by the perceptions of her childhood, she was thoroughly uninterested in putting personal events in poetry. Her goal was always to create something universal and everlasting. I wanted to be true to history, to pieces of personal existence that would be a record of what happened to one woman in one time. If a fragment of one of my poems was the only thing left of me after a nuclear holocaust, I hoped that the reader who found it would think, *So, this was what it was like for her at that time in that moment.* If a fragment of one of Phillis's poems was the only thing left, she hoped her reader would think, *Yes, this is what it's like now and forever, human and the same.* I wanted to make something else of the material of my life the same way complex tapestries are made from basic wool, shorn from sheep, washed, strung, and carded into raw material, then woven into the complex expression of tapestry. I have often felt Phillis to be the more "real" poet, though, the one whose very first poem in her very first book unfolded so elegantly, the one whose ambition was to write works that last forever, the one who only wrote poetry. By comparison, my poems could seem energetically disheveled. Besides, I also wrote prose, and reveled in doing that, too.

3.

Just out of my marriage, "graduated" temporarily from the psychotherapy that would palliate my post-traumatic stress disorder and armed with the revelations of what happened to me when, in situation after situation, I played and re-played my family designated role of rescuer, I spent that year learning to claim a great deal of time alone. The inspired poet Tom Sleigh, with whom I soon fell in love, helped me in this regard because he fiercely guarded his own time, refusing to schedule even a dentist appointment before 1pm. Often in the evenings I went to bed with a book, Paul Fussell's *Poetic Meter and Poetic Form*. At that time, free verse was the dominant mode; craft classes were a thing of the far future.

Slowly, after I realized that no one was going to teach me formal techniques at Hopkins, I began to teach myself how to write with rhyme schemes and rhythms, learning what my future friend Rachel Hadas (who was raised by a famous classics scholar father and who'd already taken Robert Fitzgerald's famous prosody course at Harvard) knew very well. The 1970s were a hostile environment for formal poetry: poets favored plain vocabulary and free-verse line breaks that chopped up sentences. Forms in poetry were considered reactionary and snooty. The poet-critic Peter Stitt called this time, "the barren days of the plainstyle."[5] I dug almost archeologically through anthologies and compendiums for formal poems, dazzled by their richness. Rummaging through a used bookstore in Washington, DC, I exhumed a blue-and-yellow hardcover Oxford volume, *A Book of Sonnets* by Robert Nye.

It was like being on the Sutton Hoo dig, unearthing sonnets as if they were enamel buckles from long-ago seafarers.

For many of my contemporaries, the line was only good for one thing—breaking. All the emphasis seemed to be on the end of the line. But what about the middle? I pawed over some of my favorite lines, looking for the secrets of their remarkably still sense of wholeness, yet their simultaneous ability to catapult the poem forward. Even something simple like Howard Nemerov's "People are putting up storm windows now," or Edna St. Vincent Millay's "and rise and sink and rise and sink again," or Shelley's "Ozymandias" barking, "Look on my Works, ye Mighty, and despair!" had a rhythmic and syntactic integrity that thrilled me.

I wonder now what would have happened if some ideologue in a workshop had told Nemerov to break the line between "putting" and "up"? Or instructed Millay to break her line after the third "and"? Or tried to con Shelley into believing that the sentence should govern his flow—break it after the second comma?

I realized I could lock in the line with a rhyme, catapulting emphasis back on the whole line with that sound, even if I hid the sound behind some very ordinary word like "was." A rhyme scheme, seemingly emphasizing the end of a line, threw weight back into the middle, the way a stevedore standing at the edge of a ship throws cargo into the hold. I marveled at how this helped the energy of a poem both backwards and forwards. If I could hide a rhyme scheme, I would have the structure without the fancy ear veneer that would mark a poem as old-fashioned. The line itself was allowing me to look backward for solutions that encouraged me to go on.[6]

"The Lull" finally stated my credo of the body as it gathered into the single stanza that often characterizes the English sonnet. It ends with half a line, like a strap slipping off a shoulder. I wrote it after my attempts in graduate school and collected it into my second book, *Raw Heaven*. Phillis also wrote sonnets, but she did not depend on them as I did—and do. Instead, she became an expert on the sonnet in a different way—but that comes later. From the ages of nine to nineteen, Phillis wrote primarily in rhyme and meter. Then she shifted to free verse in college—though she felt she was going against her nature in doing so. I, who began in free verse, felt I had found my nature in formal structures— where we are both, as mature poets, at home.

But when we first met, the poet Levin grappled with self-definition and ultimately came to write a poem that described her disembodied state. "Definition" (like "The Lull" for me) appeared in her second book. "...if I was no one/ No one could hurt me./ Does this seem ridiculous to you?" she writes in the fourth stanza. No, it doesn't seem ridiculous. It seems like a useful strategy for living for a child. To be invisible. (And to have invisible powers.)

A poet can take years to articulate a human process of becoming. A thought or observation or insight you have might well appear a decade later. *The Afterimage* wasn't published until 1995. Twenty years after graduate school, Levin's understanding of herself as an emerging adult came to exist between the pages of a book, asking a key question. "Does this seem ridiculous to you?" is not answered, really, but resolved. In Levin's "Definition" there is another unspoken query. It is *Who was I?* The poet seeks an answer not from herself, but from another, "Tell me who I am." It is a poem implying a relationship and seeking a human response, even as "The Lull" implies a relationship that won't last (I only went on one date with that person), yet gives birth to the Pax Peacock.

We are only made of flesh. "Remember to put the knives away," my mother would whisper as she left me alone with my dad, sleep tethering him like Cerberus to the couch. Our bodies, so endangered. All we have.

THE LULL
by Molly Peacock

The possum lay on the tracks fully dead.
I'm the kind of person who stops to look.
It was big and white with flies on its head,
a thick healthy hairless tail, and strong, hooked
nails on its raccoon-like feet. It was a full-
grown possum. It was sturdy and adult.
Only its head was smashed. In the lull
that it took to look, you took the time to insult
the corpse, the flies, the world, the fact that we were
traipsing in our dress shoes down the railroad tracks.
"That's disgusting." You said that. Dreams, brains, fur
and guts: what we are. That's my bargain, the Pax
Peacock, with the world. Look hard, life's soft. Life's cache
is flesh, flesh, and flesh.

DEFINITION
by Phillis Levin

I used to be ethereal:
It was my natural state
To be detached, removed, indifferent,
Not to others but to myself.

Certain things fed me: the sky, clouds,
Books, and blue flowers;
Anything red was taboo.
Now I have softened in my outlook,

And once I even wore red—
People said it was especially becoming.
They noticed me, and that's exactly
What I was avoiding.

If you could say who I was
I would die, if I was no one
No one could hurt me.
Does this seem ridiculous to you?

Of course you noticed me,
Just as we all notice a child
Who covers her face
From the glare of other eyes.

All those years I was hiding
From you, noticing so many things,
I really saw nothing at all,
Except who you were;

But you weren't hiding from me.
I thought I saw more
Because I didn't know you could see.
Now I am lost without you:

Tell me who I was.

4.

In Baltimore I lived on 37th Street, past Guilford Avenue, the borderline beyond which the university suggested a graduate student should rent, in an apartment that used to be the first floor of a house. At night from my bedroom (which had been the dining room) the lights of the police helicopters that swept the alleys beamed through once an hour. Phillis lived directly across from the university campus in an imposing brick apartment building with a doorman on Charles Street.

We had grown toward one another from opposite directions, yet somehow those opposite lines had met in lines of poetry. Phillis, whose every action was intensely examined by her mother and grandmother—they scrutinized her clothing, her elbows, the slant of her head, and almost every word she spoke—wanted only to disappear from the house with its heavy dark furniture and suffocating relationships. Because her parents lived with her widowed, maternal grandmother (in comfort but in reduced circumstances from former, more substantial wealth), they were trapped in a perpetually juvenile dyad, put in the position of the children of the powerful queen, siblings rather than husband and wife. They in turn focused their energy on their two children, Phillis and her brother. Everyone was hemmed in, and over-scrutinized. Hence my friend's longing for invisibility, her only freedom detachment from her body; and the title of her second book hints at this.

I, who after the age of ten, rarely could get the genuine attention of my parents, wanted only to become visible in the turquoise duplex house in north Buffalo that my parents, my little sister and I shared with my grandparents, uncle and aunt. Hence my feeling of being all muscle, all organ, all flesh, as I write in the sonnet, "The Lull." As a child I loved acting, and as an adult would perform in an Off-Broadway one-woman show in poems that I had written, *The Shimmering Verge*. Our sources were inversely similar wellsprings.

5.

Phillis often forgot to eat. She would write all day and never think about getting herself a meal. I'd been preparing dinners for my family since the age of twelve. I found myself cooking for other students, too, Tom and Phillis included. In feeding her, I discovered that she was an enthusiast. She loved my salads, savoring every single ingredient. She effused over every dish as if it were her first encounter with eating itself. And I, too, am a taste enthusiast. I loved greeting an experience as if it were the first time, adored re-capturing initial childhood reactions with the thrill of my perceptions—even if they led to disgust or terror. What I didn't realize at the time was that Phillis was never allowed to choose what she would eat. I, on the other hand, would dream up what I wanted to eat, and my mother would buy the ingredients, or better yet, would unexpectedly drive us to a Howard Johnson's restaurant where her friend was a waitress. It wasn't until Phillis was eighteen-years-old in college that she was faced with options and had the freedom to select her food. (For the whole first year she ate alone, uncomfortable eating with other people.)

Soon, we ventured to little Baltimore restaurants to eat fried oysters, and then to Washington, DC, to eat Pad Thai.

I was the older one, the sensible adventurer, the one who knew how to manage in life. Phillis was the sheltered one who had never learned how to ride a bicycle because it was too dangerous, yet who knew how to order a great bottle of wine. We discovered we were completely in sync as we looked at a menu. Our eyes would land on certain dishes we both instantly wanted to order. We both desired to devour too many things on every menu! Before long we realized that if we each ordered separate items for our dinner, we could share everything. (Of this, Phillis has informed every waiter at every table in every restaurant—from diner to the very occasional four star—that we've entered for the last half century.)

As we ate, we talked. We loved re-entering our earliest capabilities to perceive; we loved owning those feelings that were only ours and could never be taken away from us by challenging, threatening, fear-inducing invasive adults. We felt utterly alive in the cells of our earliest years, vital in what we touched and smelled and saw. Our talk reverberated back to my seven-year-old self, deliberating over two paint chips. Why isn't the thing its name? Just as there is a disjunction between a color and its name, so there is a disjunction between the name of a dish on a menu and the dish itself. Yet as Phillis and I sat in restaurants (being cooked for, being taken care of and mothered by a vast accumulating army of waitstaff who brought us extra plates and cutlery so that we could divide everything we'd ordered) very often the name of the dish and what was delivered were consonant. This was partly because Phillis relentlessly interrogated waiters who continually rushed back to the kitchen to unearth the answers to her questions. By the time we ordered, we knew exactly what we were getting.

"You were a grownup!" Phillis exclaims. "You had been married and divorced!" We are now seventy-five and sixty-eight, sitting in the kitchen of her stone cottage in Connecticut where she has just made me a superb omelet.

"Let's pick a year, and see where we each were," I say. We pick 1968. We were twenty and thirteen. MP was marching against the Vietnam War. PL was arguing with her parents about that war and racial equality...

6.

At home on 37th Street I was still teaching myself how to write formal verse. (This was an ongoing project that lasted well past graduate school.) Blocks away, Phillis was attempting to write free verse, despite the fact that it felt unnatural and hollow. As I worked away on shaping my poems, the issue of choosing a form for a certain subject came up. How does an impulse match a poetic form? That's something like: how does a name match a color or match a dish? Or worse, like the constant dilemma of what to title a poem. Now, after a lifetime of writing, I trust my instincts and don't even feel it as a conscious decision. But then I was thinking: is X a sonnet subject? Should the experience of Y be a villanelle? Rhyme absorbed me. I began to discover that patterned, received poetic forms like sonnets are also psychological structures. They are not exterior forms to be "filled." They are interior, the bone structure of a poem. They are a challenge to perfect, but paradoxically, they taught me that imperfection was ok in poetry. And, as such, I acquired a Winnicottian attitude toward the demands of poetic structures. I began thinking that a poet can be a "good enough mother" to a poem. You can handle a form in a "good enough" way. It is inhumane to be perfectionistic about poetic form.

Kay Ryan, reviewing the Associated Writing Programs Conference where I spoke as a last-minute add-on at a panel, notes that I said "a nice thing. She says it's wrong to think of a sonnet as a 'container' or prison; instead it is a 'skeleton,' which allows something to live and move. I can see a beautiful, animated X-ray of a galloping horse. This is a muscular and vigorous feeling about form."[7]

Many years later, I finally wrote all this into a poem, "The Flaw," crafted with the ghost of a sonnet inside its fifteen free-verse lines. I withheld the rhyme; it only starts to echo with "rug" and "nub," then "cross" buried mid-line and quietly anticipating "floss" at the end of the next line. Ten syllables give a stately sense to some lines, but other, short lines cinch the poem into sudden stops. It's like irregularly sanding wood, leaving some rough patches.

The Flaw
by Molly Peacock

The best thing about a hand-made pattern
is the flaw.
Sooner or later in a hand-loomed rug,
among the squares and flattened triangles,
a little red nub might soar above a blue field,
or a purple cross might sneak in between
the neat ochre teeth of the border.
The flaw we live by, the wrong color floss,
now wreathes among the uniform strands
and, because it does not match,
makes a red bird fly,
turning blue field into sky.
It is almost, after long silence, a word
spoken aloud, a hand saying through the flaw,
I'm alive, discovered by your eye.

I firmly believe that a poem is a handmade object. We value a poem's beauty for its flaws, just the way the price of a handmade chest of drawers goes up because an expert on *Antiques Roadshow* reveals the disguised gouge of the craftsman's slip when working a plane to create a secret drawer. In a universe of steel and glass, the handmade is a genuine relief: it's human. By the eleventh and twelfth lines of the poem, I insert a directly rhyming couplet. It sets up the connection that makes "The Flaw" into a kind of love poem, with its rhyming last line. Human makers speak through craft, especially if you've been practicing a craft long enough to be easy and poised about it.

As I developed as a formal poet, I was developing, well, forming, as a person, and that meant I had a deep interest in what made a whole person, like a whole room. I didn't feel whole. I felt I was an assemblage of parts, that I didn't have a core. But let's leave the idea of a psychological core for later—when Phillis and I, quite independently, begin living in New York. Right now, we're in Baltimore, and I'm putting ordinary North American lettuce and ordinary North American cucumbers into my shopping basket while Phillis is at the Deli counter, lost in thought, then smiling as she envelops the waitperson into the Levin Query Cloud, with question after question about the regions of Italy or France or Greece that produced the particular cheese she is pondering buying. And we're going to stay right there, freeze-framed, while I diverge a bit into the pronoun "I."

7.

For almost forty years I've made part of my living teaching poetry privately one-to-one, usually on the phone, and sometimes in person or on Zoom. My students are sophisticated, often with books published and MFA degrees. They know a lot but feel it's time to know more. In the far-ranging conversations they initiate with me, inevitably the subject of the pronoun "I" comes up. They worry about whether too much "I" will make their poems self-indulgent. I don't think so at all. Readers appreciate contact with the genuine self of the poet (not the posturing self.) A candid "I" can be a neutral witness to whatever experience the poem unfolds. When Shakespeare whines in "Sonnet 29," "in disgrace with fortune and men's eyes" he is both the whiner *and* the witness. He's the neutral observer of that outcast, envious, discontented self-hater who is also he.

> When, in disgrace with fortune and men's eyes,
> I all alone beweep my outcast state,
> And trouble deaf heaven with my bootless cries,
> And look upon myself and curse my fate,
> Wishing me like to one more rich in hope,
> Featured like him, like him with friends possessed,
> Desiring this man's art and that man's scope,
> With what I most enjoy contented least;
> Yet in these thoughts myself almost despising,

He's really wallowing in it, and it gives his readers permission to identify with all their own jealousies, and all the ways they pity themselves, wishing they were richer, or more beautiful, or had better friends (or any friends at all). That fabulous sonnet wouldn't exist without "I all alone beweep…" The sheer self-indulgence is luxurious. But even Shakespeare can't convince my students—who would never want to appear as self-absorbed whiners the way the most sublimely talented writer in English is.

The question has come up so often and has caused so much angst to so many talented writers, that I went in search of another self-discloser and self-examiner. That's how I came upon the Index of First Lines in my *Complete Poems of Emily Dickinson.* The list in the index makes a 142-line poem itself, displaying the stalwart Dickinson "I" and containing some of her most arresting first lines. The "I"-lines comprise a twelfth of the 1775 poems in her *Complete Poems.* Why erase the self? So much of poetry is about declaring one. If the two subjects of lyric poetry are love and death, is not identity (a word beginning with the letter I) the thing that anchors love and that we memorialize in death? Many of Dickinson's openings pair the pronoun with the simplest verbs of being and perceiving: am, cannot, could, felt, had, know, saw, think, was. As an exercise for myself, I once collaged some of those lines in alphabetical order, just to demonstrate how forceful and musical a claim to identity can be—or, as Dickinson wrote, "I took my Power in my Hand—"[8]

Chapter Three:
Careful of Each Other

1.

Phillis and I squashed into a little booth made of soft yellow plastic anchored by metal grommets on West 19th St and 7th Avenue. It was 1981 in New York City, four years after we graduated. She was working on her first book; mine was just published. In this Asian-Latin fusion diner, long closed now, we were eating seared string beans—seared so hot, their skins became partly translucent. Used to the stolid green beans of my grandmother's garden, the dish suddenly made me realize that bean skins grew in layers—but of course they do. Everything in life is layered if you just look closely enough. One link in our friendship, and one layer of my developing aesthetic, had grown because of Richard Howard.

At the Writing Seminars we'd been students of the Pulitzer-prize winning poet and translator who, at fifty, had just begun his teaching career. Being in New York, though I rarely saw him there, made me feel at home in Richard's territory. He was the first true person of letters I had ever met, a poetry kingmaker who seemed to pop up on every prize committee and editorial board. Richard might have seemed cruel to those in the literary world who felt his power, but underneath his arched eyebrows, behind his dramatically huge round red glasses, and above his thin red tie and impeccable beard, his eyes took us seriously. He was thoughtful, warm, and motherly, if sometimes explosively unpredictable. A classmate described him as a Volcano God in a black and white Hollywood B movie. She would leave her manuscript outside his door as if it were a platter of fruit and flowers meant to placate Richard's rumbling. But Phillis and I soaked up his attention.

In the exclusive *tête-à-tête* hour I had with him as part of our seminar, he read my poems with laser focus and said, "Dear, these poems are all carried forth on the force of pure emotion. What are you going to do when that force isn't there?" I did not have an answer to that. He didn't expect me to. How the question rang for me was that a.) I couldn't believe I'd ever run out of the force of emotion and b.) but what if I did? What if that was part of the poet's growing up? Where was the underpinning that might move my poems forward? I had an inkling of an answer on my nightstand with the Fussell book on form and Babette Deutsch's *A Poetry Handbook*.

Richard had asked me one of the key questions of my aesthetic life. I knew that he would rarely have time for me and that I was lucky to get his attention when I did. Yet when he turned to me, it was with his full absorption. One of the reasons I could receive the ample nourishment of his rare responses was that I knew he would never be sexually interested in me. Our exchanges were purely in the realm of the mind. Giving this a neurological twist: how could I structure my brain to poetically process my experiences?

Phillis, who decided to go into a PhD program in English Literature at The CUNY Graduate Center instead of entering a program in clinical psychology, had rented a little 250-square foot apartment on West 13th Street between Sixth and Seventh Avenues in the Village, not far from where Richard lived. But after my year in Baltimore, I went on to live in Wilmington Delaware, as Poet-in-Residence for that tiny three-county state, working for the Arts Council till my first book came out, in 1981. I felt stuck in Delaware. When Richard encouraged me to apply for an Ingram Merrill fellowship and I was awarded one, I used it to finance my leap to New York City, to a studio apartment in a mid-rise building on East 71st Street with a blue elevator—so blue, with its round metal window, that it looked like an aquarium.

Richard gave me a model of a life outside of academe, yet within the poetry world. Though he taught us in Baltimore, he was not a full-time professor. He lived in New York, where he wrote and translated in a high-ceilinged studio apartment with walls full of books and photographs—including photos of Auden in the bathroom! Small space, big reputation. He would open a stuffed closet and drag out a Bloomingdale's bag full of fresh, hardcover poetry books: the visitor, me, got to choose a handful of these beauties he didn't have room for, either on his shelves or in his head, and I walked away, adding to my own slender poetry library.

2.

After I found a studio apartment on the upper Eastside, Phillis and I began sharing meals and exchanging poems. That's how we ended up eating string beans and doing what we've continued to do in restaurants over time: exchanging and mulling and exclaiming and pondering over our typed or carbon-copy poems with handwritten arrows in pencil on the typed copy or pen scrawled on the carbon. I graduated to xerox copies as soon as I found the least-used hours at the

Religious Society of Friends offices. Friends Seminary faculty had some copying privileges. And Phillis used a copy place in the Village near Stevdan's, our beloved stationery store on Sixth Avenue.

From the translucent skin on a seared string bean to the smooth, soothing heartiness of spaetzle, to chunky borscht, sharing a meal with Phillis meant sharing a delight in detail amidst a barrage of free association. Phillis would open her mouth as we sat down, and a torrent of language would come toward me like a weather front. The waitperson would return again and again to take our order, and we wouldn't be ready. In desperation I would yelp, "Fifteen minutes of silence, Phillis!"

"Oh," she would say, and quiet down. I had drawn a boundary. We perused the menu. Menus, with their long lists, look a little bit like poems on laminated pages. Though Phillis had grown up with many seemingly specific and therefore crisp-boundaried requirements, paradoxically, her experience felt boundaryless because her parents intruded with constant questions and continual criticisms. "You read too much, you write too much, you THINK too much!" she recalls her father screaming. Yet they left her alone for many hours to set up scientific experiments with magnets and a bottle of mercury, to read Kafka, Woolf, and Freud from her parents' extensive library, and to create scenes with Allie the marble in the basement of their house.

Curiously, my family had a different kind of boundary-lessness. My mother felt from when I was quite small that I was adult enough to make decisions most little girls don't get to make exclusively, like deciding what to wear with what and when to wear it, what we should all eat, what color my sister's and my room should be, how much money I needed for school. She let me make massive fashion errors (prints and stripes with plaids) both out of feeling a child should own an environment and out of a kind of neglect at those times when she sank into her own depressed world. (In New Jersey Phillis couldn't choose what she wore; her mother laid her clothes out on her bed.)

Later my mother depended on me to make decisions no burgeoning girl should ever have been allowed to make. Like charging me, at twelve, to be responsible for my nine-year-old sister, alone in our house while my mother worked long hours. Other kids had rules: an allowance, for instance, or a curfew. I had no set rules until I got to college. She expected me to behave, and I did behave—by being constantly watchful and picking up cues from the environment as to what it was appropriate for me to say and do. I got very good at anticipating which adult behavior was correct in a situation. I was intuitive and could read other people and even read a room very quickly, picking up the intensity of real emotions behind facades.

As I think back, I realized I developed boundaries because my father projected not only an aura of violence, but one of incest. He did not sexually abuse me, but he lived in the drunken cloud of an unpredictable man stomping about in his underwear. To make sure that I wasn't invaded personally, or that my room wasn't invaded (a room I carefully decorated and that was never destroyed by him as he broke the furniture and hurled the objects in the kitchen and living room), I developed quite a thick metaphorical wall around myself. Beginning with puberty, as I was cooking for my father and sister, responsible for her, whom I loved and resented, even as I loved and hated my father, supervising her homework, ironing his shirts, nagging him to get off the couch and get to work, I developed a very strong outer layer, the thing that allowed me to achieve and be editor of the school yearbook, but never was allowed the internal time, the freedom, to develop a core. The length of that previous sentence gives an idea of my state of mind. Developing that core was what I later did, for many years, in psychotherapy.

I intuited how much Phillis needed conversational boundaries, and I was quite matter-of-fact, and occasionally even would tell her to shut up. Which she, recalibrating, would do. It was just a way to break an overheated cycle. As a daughter in a household where we were supposed to pretend things were "normal," never naming my dad's alcoholism or questioning his behavior, I got used to not asking questions, but gleaning information from unspoken clues—like counting how many empty beer bottles might yield degrees of wildness. As a result, I was a non-intrusive, intuitively empathic friend. In turn, Phillis recognized vulnerabilities in me. She understood that while I was overdeveloped in logistical skills and people skills ("I was in awe of your organization!" she marvels), that my own core was just beginning to form.

We were careful of each other.

3.

We never "critiqued" one another's poems. Let me repeat that, we capital N, never critiqued one another's poems. We *showed* them to one another with our coffee or tea in the Ukrainian National Home on First Avenue where large-breasted, large-bellied grandmotherly waitresses brought us chunky borscht, or at Tea and Sympathy on Greenwich Avenue where a harried British hipster brought our cucumber sandwiches, or at Ideal German Restaurant on East 86th Street in Yorkville, near my neighborhood, where an energetic, efficiently thin woman in an apron, with hair drawn back, delivered our meatballs. *Oh, look what you did in this line!* We might say to one another. *That's interesting*, Phillis would say and then suddenly start quoting a philosopher she had read. Phillis has a kind of thesaurus of alternative words in her mind. I have a sense of sequence, a narrative instinct. Phillis's instinct is completely lyrical—not grounded in narrative at all. But syntax is central to us both.

Inclinations and talents differed. But our ambition was the same. We wanted to finish poems. We wanted to send them out to the best places (all print journals then, like *The Paris Review, The New Republic, The Nation, Poetry, The New Yorker,* of course, and two Canadian journals I respected, *The Malahat Review* and *The Fiddlehead*). We wanted our poems noticed. And we thought we were wonderful poets. Neither of us had very much money in those days. We found ourselves eating grilled cheese sandwiches at Joe Jr.'s Coffee Shop on Sixth Avenue. If we had enough cash, we might spring for an Italian meal at Gene's in the West Village or Lanza's in the East Village, both restaurants so old that the style of serving and the menus would have existed in our parents' day. We were ecstatic at the rectangular dishes of crudités that would appear on the white tablecloth at Gene's, the celery hearts, the carrot sticks, and the sublimely knife-cut radish roses.

Even though we were extremely ambitious, we did not talk about achievements or about what we were going to do to get where we wanted to be. It was unspoken, but absolutely clear, that we could have turned into rivals. There could have been a competitive edge to our exchange, but instinctively, protectively, we refused it. Phillis, who aimed to see the best in everyone and the best in everything, was sometimes ridiculously naive. On the other hand, I, too, was shockingly naive, once leaving my purse open on a chair beside me, and finding it later in a nearby garbage can, the money gone and the purse itself filled with urine, from which I had to fish out my driver's license, because the thought of standing in line to replace it was worse than the prospect of the pee. (As she re-read this paragraph, Phillis corrected me. "I was innocent," she said. "There's a difference between innocence and naiveté.")

4.

Unlike Phillis, I am not shy. My father gave me courage. Not through his upstanding example, but because he was so violent and unpredictable in his affection that cowering in my room would only invite his destruction. It was far better to go out and stand as tall as a fourteen-year-old can stand and be a disapproving witness to the demolition of the furniture. (A teenage girl can be simultaneously afraid and censorious.) Largely it worked; he never came after me if I was already there in the room, actively watching him. He needed me more as a witness to his frustration than as a victim. My courage to be there—I now think I was there *for* him—gave me a sense of power, something that is essential for a person to become a confident writer.

While Mr. Levin, with his mechanical pencil clipped to his shirt pocket, was discussing algebra, geometry, and electricity with his daughter, Mr. Peacock, a pencil behind his ear, taught me the carpenter's lexicon of flatheads, Phillips, and Robertsons. Tools = craft. Shop = studio.

Unlike my Dad, with his brushcut, long dead from his drinking, Phillis's father, even as a nonagenarian, was still sharp and an inspiration to her. He was an accomplished mechanical and electronics engineer and encouraged her life of the mind. "The mind, mind has mountains," Gerard Manley Hopkins says in his desolate sonnet. "The mind is an enchanted thing, an enchanting thing," Marianne Moore says in her eponymously titled poem, and both of us believe this with our whole hearts. Yet Phillis tells me her father was afraid of her intellectual propensities. "What are you, an intellectual nut?" he'd ask her. It led us to consider our precocious minds. In retrospect, we realize how much our precocity threatened our fathers (and Phillis's mother, who had been a brilliant student), though it made my mother proud. Many adults, and for me that includes some teachers, were afraid of us.

Both of us had reasons to escape into our heads. Phillis went to hers willingly, toward thought processes which would enable her to understand the world that remained unspoken in the maternal side of her family, who, with their wealth and intelligence and sophistication, had escaped Europe several generations before the Holocaust, establishing themselves in the silk capital of the New World, Paterson, New Jersey—not to mention the nearby locale of William Carlos Williams in Rutherford. Phillis had received an award judged by the poet Louis Ginsberg, Allen Ginsberg's father, and eventually she got to know Allen, as I later did. Her father's family came from Reading, PA, birthplace of Wallace Stevens. The idea of an "interior paramour," as Stevens puts it, who lights the mind, "how high that highest candle lights the dark," was almost present for Phillis when she was just a zygote.

A talented child's attitude toward the body also creates the ground for aesthetic decisions later on. Just as Phillis detached from her body, wishing to be invisible, domestic danger compelled me to be visible at all costs. A childhood strategy for living becomes an adult aesthetic approach if that kid is talented and goes on to develop a gift, as the two of us did, so far apart from one another, me wearing a hand-made gathered skirt (that was too short for my lanky legs so was let down, the hemline covered in rickrack by my very dexterous grandmother), and Phillis in her Kimberly School forest green jacket with the embroidered insignia and pleated skirt. And those strategies now were surfacing in the ways we constructed our poems and talked about them in restaurants: over tomato soup in Elephant and Castle with its black-and-white menu, or on a special occasion—one of our birthdays?—having tea at the Pierre Hotel. Below the ceiling painted with putti, me in my black silk blouse with tiny magenta trapezoid shapes in the print, Phillis in her black blazer, went over every line in the typescripts we brought until each poem had been thoroughly appreciated, thought about, *read*.

There's both a childhood aspect of parallel play and an aspect of parental mirroring to our process. "Tabula Rasa," a poem from Levin's collection *Mr. Memory & Other Poems*, has a haunting image of mirroring. A child is trying to get a glimpse of what's inside a mirror without seeing herself (something like trying to take a photo of a scene with a mirror in it and angling yourself out of the reflection). By the fourth stanza we realize that the child is in her parents' bedroom, and the mirror must be their bedroom mirror. Beside the bepillowed bed are drawers with adult treasures or mysteries, like Trojans. The hunger to go into the world of the mirror, which is the realm of fairy tale, drives the poem. Inside the reflection, the startling, dangerous reality of adult sexuality appears. After all the calm description come the final terrifying lines:

> To see not myself in the mirror but the mirror
> Itself, a white wolf with its pink tongue panting.

TABULA RASA
by Phillis Levin

To see not herself in the mirror but the mirror itself,
Startled by starlings, darlings of the eye, apples
At home in their lunar glow, piano scales
Welling below, with nobody near except

This child determined to gaze at a surface unyielding
Yet ever-fluctuating, giving in to every whim of light,
Giving in not at all to her wish, her will to be
Unseen. And why did she want this? Though I

Am she I cannot tell, can only say
Her desire was born starkly, bare-boned and mute,
Tiptoeing, flagrant—to face a giant nothingness
Full of family secrets, icy, molten,

Taciturn, unknown. Look at her trying to steal
A look without getting caught in the glass,
Betrayed again by a sliver of flesh, a quiver of
Self-sight. Here is the bed of the mother and father,

Island of sheets and pillows, Persian blue velvet,
Apricot silk, here the bureau of many drawers
(In one, under a packet of letters, Trojans
Asleep in their wrappers), a comb and a brush

Waiting to touch the prince and princess, perfumes
Growing old in their vials, baroque filigree stems...
To see not myself in the mirror but the mirror
Itself, a white wolf with its pink tongue panting.

Danger and terror. That last line is so shocking. You never
know, writing a poem, what you will come to, what will
surprise you: an image that will clarify. The mirroring we
received from our parents had distortions. The reflection
of the world back to us as children was not exactly like
a funhouse mirror, but it was rippled. Behind our urges
to write was a seeking of a true image. That last image in
"Tabula Rasa," where "the white wolf" suddenly appears, is
terrifyingly intrusive, and true. "The pink tongue panting"
so alliteratively has the adult sexual truth in it but also the
shocking color of terror itself. The image bursts out of the
boundaries of the poem.

How is it that our own interchanges remained so boundaried and pristine? Ritual. Like the ritual of a hotel afternoon tea itself. Our custom is ceremonial, comprised of food with a postscript of silently reading words on paper, then bursts of our responses and associations with very gentle ideas, never critiques. It's got an aura of sacrament, though I don't want to get too religious here. Let's say these exchanges combine my desire to feel what I am feeling and not to delay it, to be completely present, with Phillis's presence, she who sometimes requires three or four or ten years to process emotions and declares that slow processing is simply part of her nature. "I usually feel things right away but don't have words for them," Phillis says to me. "The poems feel what I don't feel or know till later."

"How can I explain to people that we don't critique each other?" I asked Phillis when she had read this part of what I've written.

"Say it's like a studio visit," she said.

After the Pierre waiter explained that we should pay our check because his shift was coming to an end, after the tearoom had completely emptied out except for us, talking and talking about images and syntax at our table which was like our studio, finally it was time to retrieve our coats and walk out into the pitch dark where the air was cold, and the lights were on, and the traffic crawled down Fifth Avenue.

Chapter Four:
A Poet's Self-Portrait: John Clare

1.

I am still mulling over Phillis's distinction between innocence and naiveté. "I wasn't naive, because I was canny about people. I was innocent because I had no guile," she amplified for me. Could it be that innocence is intimately connected to intuition, while naiveté refers to an ignorance of the social world? And do these qualities connect to aesthetic identity? Is innocence connected to absence of language? It brings me back to the personal pronoun.

British Romantic poet John Clare wrote a poem dominated by a personal pronoun, "I Am" at Northampton County Asylum, where Clare was confined for his last twenty-two years. The fact that we even have "I Am" at all is due to the house-steward of that asylum, W. F. Knight, who copied out Clare's poetry and saved it.

I AM
by *John Clare (1793–1864)*

I am—yet what I am, none cares or knows;
    My friends forsake me like a memory lost:
I am the self-consumer of my woes;
    They rise and vanish in oblivion's host,
Like shadows in love's frenzied stifled throes:
And yet I am, and live—like vapours toss't

Into the nothingness of scorn and noise—
    Into the living sea of waking dreams,
Where there is neither sense of life or joys,
    But the vast shipwreck of my life's esteems;
Even the dearest, that I love the best
Are strange—nay stranger than the rest.

I long for scenes where man hath never trod
    A place where woman never smiled or wept
There to abide with my Creator, God,
    And sleep as I in childhood sweetly slept,
Untroubling, and untroubled where I lie,
The grass below—above the vaulted sky.[9]

Unlike his contemporaries, the British Romantic poets
Keats, Shelley, Wordsworth and Byron, Clare was a poor
farm laborer whose mother struggled to have him in school
a few months a year, at least until he was thirteen and had
to go to work. The poet, Carolyn Kizer tells us in her introduction to her selection of his poems, *The Essential Clare,*
not only managed to read, but to read widely and well,
from the Elizabethan poets through his contemporaries,
and to write extraordinary poems. He loved Pope and another poet who was out of favor in his time—John Donne.

By his early teens, Kizer explains, he was writing ballads and showing them to his parents, who laughed at them until Clare claimed he'd copied them from a book—as the asylum steward would copy Clare's own poems decades later. Clare had many jobs, among them bartender at the Blue Bell pub, and many hours of farm work and intense family life—a wife and seven children plus his parents in a tiny cottage. But his chief occupation was walking in the countryside where he observed birds and wrote poems about their habits and their nests.

Miraculously, Clare managed to compile a book of poems called *Poems Descriptive of Rural Life and Scenery* which was published when he was twenty-seven. (My first book was published in 1981; Phillis's was in 1988. We both were thirty-four—seven years apart.) Kizer mentions that Clare's book sold 4,000 copies in its first year. Most North American first books sell less than a quarter of that. (Shelley's first book sold only about 500 copies.) Of course, Clare had to travel to London where the book was launched. And he suffered the way every author does—what was he going to wear? He wore what he had, of course, his country clothes. He went to the fancy gatherings in his bright green farmer's coat. He shook hands with Coleridge and de Quincey in his bright green coat. He ate London delicacies in his bright green coat. The bumpkin who sold eight times as well as Shelley was an easy mark in this outerwear. Critics called him "the green man." He probably looked like he stepped off a package of frozen vegetables. But all book tours come to their ends, and Clare was soon back home. Not only did he need to support his own wife and children, but his parents. As well, Clare suffered from bouts of fen ague, a type of malaria. These episodes began to break his physical health. More devastating were his mental breakdowns.

2.

Who knows how Clare would have made out if someone had offered him a Danforth fellowship? But while Shelley romped through Europe and Wordsworth paced at home, the green man Clare was put away. (The local asylum, according to Kizer, wasn't the snake pit one might imagine. The poet actually had some out-patient privileges, thanks to his saving relationship with the warden.) Though most poets tap into extremes of emotion, they are also tapped by the emotions generated by their time and place—which, paradoxically, can produce timelessness and placelessness. "I Am" may have been written in an institution, but that place itself figures nowhere. The literal tradeoff for residence in the asylum was that Clare was well fed and physically healthy—and he wrote. People debate the quality of his late poems, but no one doubts the power of "I Am." It is the self-assessment of a lonesome, but wise man. Clare must have suffered terribly from his seclusion, but he also must have suffered from the close quarters of his family. "I Am" defines itself by a longing for identity-affirming solitude:

> *I am—yet what I am, none cares or knows;*

The insistence that we *are*, that we exist, and therefore have a right to our existence is so basic to our idea of living it almost doesn't need to be articulated—except by someone whose existence is challenged daily, perhaps hourly, by his state of mind.

In a richly obvious alternating rhyme scheme, Clare explores the reality of his state.

> *My friends forsake me like a memory lost:*
> *I am the self-consumer of my woes;*

To be forsaken, lost, in effect to be erased—Clare's identity is challenged by the kind of oblivion the absence of free human contact imposes. He describes those woes as they *rise and vanish* like shadows in *frenzied stifled throes* then re-asserts, *And yet I am, and live.* "I Am" is about what can never be suppressed, in spite of all the ways society and the self conspire to jail it: the essence of who a person is, or *sawol*, the Old English root of soul.

When a sentence winds around lines, then bridges the gap between stanzas, its syntax has a special plasticity. Only one sentence in Clare's poem extends from the first line through the first two whole stanzas, stretched by the elegant use of semi-colons and dashes through twelve whole lines. Into the *nothingness* Clare calls *scorn and noise*—referring to the strange insubstantiality of the things that heavily stress us—which is also part of

> *the living sea of waking dreams*
> *where there is neither sense of life or joys...*

The ship of the self plunges. The poet underpaints a vast pulsing horizon of waking dreams, and in this state of moving, plankton-like neutrality the ship of *my life's esteems* comes to the disaster of its *vast shipwreck*, where the world inverts.

How many of us, when our world is belly-up, have stared at our families and thought, "They are complete strangers!" (And, Phillis said to me, "Are we not strangers to them, too?")

> *Even the dearest, that I love the best*
> *Are strange—nay stranger than the rest.*

Whimsically, Clare plays on stranger with *nay stranger than the rest.* Part of the sanity of this poem lies in its vigorously playful nature, always taking time to insure the delivery of its puns and simple rhymes like *best* and *rest*. If artistically you can deliver, then a kind of deliverance will be at hand just from the intensity of your making.

The quest for solitude, which in this self-portrait parallels—or perhaps actually *is*—the quest for identity, blooms in the last stanza.

> *I long for scenes where man hath never trod*
> *A place where woman never smiled or wept*

The Latin root of solitude means *alone, single, or one only.* I think again of his cramped cottage and of his wife, Patty Turner (whom he married seven months pregnant, Carolyn Kizer tells us, after he became estranged from his childhood love, Mary Joyce, the daughter of a farmer too prosperous for the Clare clan).

3.

To be alone is to recognize an individuality that can be lost in the manyness of too much company. We live in a crowded world, a noisome, clamoring place, where our attention is constantly diverted from our stream of being. I know people who do nothing but *respond* all day. They are so tuned to respond that their ability to follow their own course is as drained of intention as a dry leaf. A person's oneness, the fully integrated essence of who we are, gathered, and fully alive—that's the state Levin and Peacock longed for. To know who we are is to know why we are living.

Solitude, Clare says, means to be alone *within* the universe, *at one*, with the grass below and *the vaulted sky* above, *connected*.

There to abide with my Creator, God,
And sleep as I in childhood sweetly slept,
Untroubling, and untroubled where I lie,
The grass below – above the vaulted sky.

His last image of the child sleeping reminds me of the Child Pose in yoga—a pose of rest, "untroubled," and therefore no trouble to anyone, the child sweetly positioned between earth and sky, security below and freedom above. To sleep without interruption (think of the noise of Clare's household, and the noise of the asylum, and his longing to tramp the natural world of nests and birds, and to be sexual, of course, making physical links to all the universe) is also to be at one, to find the God within.

We might call the Creator that moving force of creativity within ourselves, what allows us to be the makers, the *scops*, of our lives. That childlike state that the Romantics knew so much about, the place of innocence that I'm calling intuition, makes quiet attention achievable.[10]

Chapter Five
The Saturday Ritual

1.

Ronald Reagan was in office. The Religious Society of Friends was working for Nuclear Disarmament. Every day I was aware that the soft purple purse I carried felt flimsy as a plastic bag compared to the classic Coach leather crossbodies on the mothers of the students I taught at Friends Seminary. The lineup for Woody Allen's *Hannah and Her Sisters* circled for blocks on the Upper West Side. My closest gay friend, in a spasm of anxiety, was about to be tested for HIV. I was in credit card debt. My accountant refused to believe that the income I declared from Friends Seminary was the only income I had. Well, I did have that extra $100 I earned from the poem I published in *The New Yorker*....

In a beautiful confluence, the same therapist who had helped me so much in Binghamton, New York, Joan Stein, had also moved to New York City. I began to see her again, thanks to the incredible insurance policy offered by Friends Seminary to their underpaid faculty. Twice a week I took the subway to lie on the couch and cry in the living room on

West 72nd Street that was also her home office. Every week she asked about how I was writing and what I was managing to send out. I lay there prone, weeping, and whining that all my time was consumed by the endless demands of the twelve-year-olds and their parents, the teachers, the principal, and the fact that I had to get up so early to get downtown to school that I had no morning time to write a poem. (Occasionally, I rose to blow my nose.) No matter what I did, the school depleted me.

Yet teaching seventh grade let me watch the normal development of twelve-year-olds—the exact age when I was called upon to be an unprepared, unlikely adult. It helped to watch them. Observing their behaviors let me think back to my own—and see the injustice of my bewildered, helpless parents' decisions.

In the Friends Seminary Middle School, I could hide. I could spend my time with the kids' elastic brains, not having to assign grades, and inventing wild assignments, hoping to instill creative habits that might just last a lifetime for them. Then, I could write new poems and polish a collection in the two and half months of cherished vacation in the summer.

Meanwhile Phillis lived her downtown life and worked on her poems and graduate courses.

Periodically, I'd get a phone call from one of my sister's boyfriends that she had gone crazy again. Drunk and drugged, the tawny beauty was breaking up barstools in Woodstock, New York. I'd learned not to be guilted by the boyfriends, and I'd refuse to go get her. I knew by the time I got up to Woodstock, it would be all over, and then what? Just the trip back to New York where I devoted myself to my young charges and also, somehow, had to fit in the time to write. But how could I, an exclusively hypnogogic poet, the kind who has to write a poem in bed before I'm fully awake, make time for that important early-morning state in my chaotic schedule of poor sleep, alarm clocks, early school openings, and subway breakdowns?

It was time for me to create the time to create.

I worked out the strategy on Joan Stein's couch. The Saturday Ritual would begin on Thursday. Monday, Tuesday, and Wednesday, I decided, I would devote to the school exclusively. But after lunch on Thursday, I would start thinking of my poem. Not working the whole thing out in my head (though Phillis sometimes did that), just getting a vague idea that could waft in my mind, not to focus on, but to be aware of, while I was teaching. On Friday, I came to school planning to be there in body only. My mind was in the poem. Yet I wasn't writing it; I was aware of what it would look and feel like—often a received form, like a sonnet. The kids would be writing. Friday was creative writing day, or, if I really wanted it easy, a spelling or grammar quiz. I held the inchoate, wordless poem in my head as I paced the aisles giving the kids help, or enunciating the spelling words for the quiz. I didn't eat lunch with my colleagues. I left the building and ate alone in a booth in a coffee shop.

At 3:15 I departed from the school and took the Third Avenue bus that crawled uptown to where I lived. On the way home I bought groceries and heaved them into the elevator and into my tiny kitchen. And after I ate what I cooked myself for dinner (I had a thing for chicken livers and onions, then, and ate them with a mélange of artichoke hearts, spring peas, and mushrooms—with a chocolate ice cream chaser), I got out the vacuum cleaner and cleaned my apartment. I had already refused my boyfriend Friday nights. He could not sleep over. I went nowhere and did nothing but my domestic tasks. Even if I was so tired that I fell asleep after work and ended up vacuuming at midnight, I tidied and cleaned. I was going to wake up on Saturday with a full refrigerator and an orderly house and a sense of time unfolding like a meadow. And then, on Saturday morning I would prop myself up in bed and write that poem that could materialize from my head into words.

If I did this every week, I'd have fifty poems by the end of the year (two weeks off for holidays.) I could throw half of them away and still have half a book written. It never quite worked out to that many poems because on some Saturdays I woke up with ideas for revisions of previous poems, but such was my ritual.

And poems came in one long breath. Neither Phillis nor I take long to write a poem; Phillis reminds me that she gets a poem down in ten or so minutes. (She composes first in memory and often has her opening and closing lines before the rest of it.) As for me, I cannot let a poem continue after any sort of break. I have to write it whole, then and there. A sonnet takes me at the very most between forty-five minutes and an hour. But it requires wide open space on either side of that hour to have the presence of mind to allow the poem to arrive. And it may take days, weeks, or years to make the necessary connections to finish the poem. That's the work of it.

Though Phillis could revise her poems, I kept wrecking mine with over-revision. When I finally hit upon the Saturday ritual, producing a poem almost every week, I didn't have the pressure to produce substantial revisions. I could just abandon the ones that weren't successful. (Or put them in a folder labeled "Maybe" to be rarely opened.) The more I wrote, the more fluid and expert the poems became—and the tenderer I became. Sometimes I wrote in tears. My second book, published in 1984, was all sonnets or sonnet-like poems.

The Saturday ritual worked on so many levels. In those early years, I practiced it out of necessity. Later, I would come to have more time to write—and probably could've abandoned the practice. But I often still write a poem on Saturday. Habits make a destiny.

2.

In the lucky summers, when we had the good fortune to be accepted, both Phillis and I went to artists' retreats. MacDowell in Peterborough, NH—with its combination of woods and farmland meadows, as well as studios built especially for composers, poets, novelists, painters, sculptors, and filmmakers—still had the vibe of the early twentieth-century community of artists it was born from. It was a kind of forest bathing—and it was like a summer cruise, electric with sexual encounters. We never went to the same artists' retreat at the same time, but for both of us, these places felt like being held in the hands of a more than good enough mother. All our needs were taken care of. We were fed, we were housed, and the only line to the outside world was a pay phone booth which you stood in line for hours to use. The farmhouse where I had a bedroom smelled of my grandparents' house. The studios I was assigned to smelled of fireplace wood. It was a living Poetics of Space on 450 acres.

Both Phillis and I tried to incorporate the work habits we developed at art residencies into our writing habits in the working world. Writing poems allowed us to breathe inside the demands of our work—and writing also allowed us to avoid the consequences of psychological triggers. It's not metaphorical: working at a poem creates a physical respiration inside the writer. Even as a child Phillis recognized this: as her father and mother screamed at each other, as her brother cried helplessly, as her mother insisted that Phillis couldn't leave for school until she swallowed the mixture of raw egg and milk that was supposed to nourish her, as her grandmother rose from deep in the chairs in the darkened rooms, swinging the keys to doors only she could unlock, Phillis almost forgot how to breathe. But writing a poem allowed her to respire. For me, an artists' retreat was a physical embodiment of safety. It was a place where I wasn't endangered. No one would have to tell me to put all the knives away because, you never know, your drunken father might plunge one into your chest. At an artists' retreat, I could perform a twist on Wordsworth's "emotion recollected in tranquility": terror recollected in safety. The soft woods and meadows let me remember and reintegrate shock and distress. In the breezes of those summers, poems billowed like sheets on the line.

3.

The Poetry Society of America on Gramercy Park is not far from Friends Seminary on Rutherford Place, both secret green squares in New York, historical and magical. Back from MacDowell or Yaddo, I started volunteering at the PSA. Soon a position on the Board opened up; I volunteered for that, too. The director left. I volunteered to interview candidates. Elise Paschen was chosen, and we started to collaborate. An enrolled member of the Osage nation, a Harvard graduate whose mother was a famous ballerina, lean, athletic, with a cloud of tawny hair, Elise was a cool girl who could work a room. She modeled for me how to sail through a crowd. I hope I modeled how to shoulder into a problem and work till you dropped. We became happy collaborators, project-friends, and because of our own combination of inclinations, a cultural institution was born: Poetry in Motion on New York's subways and buses. Elise wanted to do for poetry in New York what London had done with Poetry on the Underground. I wanted to bring poetry to the guys with metal lunchboxes riding the subways, men like my father, who mocked poetry because they were locked out of it by elites.

I was part of those elites, sort of. But I carried my background, those blue-collar workers and farmers I came from, inside me—and sometimes, it felt that I was carrying them on my back, especially as my father died, as my sister entered a methadone program, as my mother sold her grocery store and began to work in a hospital. I hurtled myself forward into achievement after achievement. To stay bound to them made me feel I would die. I was inside the Anglo-Saxon riddle, flying with the birds, swimming in the seas, diving under the waves, and dying with the fishes. In some ways I really did die with the fishes, because a person can't lead an arts organization without making enemies (without even knowing it, just in expressing my opinions, in being myself, smarty-pants from a public school who could really write poetry and make savvy arts admin decisions, too). I never wanted to leave anyone out and worked to open up the membership of the Poetry Society for all poetry lovers—stopping the elaborate application process. I was making enemies of those who loved hierarchies. I was a woman, and I was running things.

And something else had happened: one of the young men who later became one of the most distinguished editors, writers and translators of his age, Jonathan Galassi, had chosen my second book to publish at Random House. He sent the book to every influential poet. It was laconic, tender-hearted Jonathan who allowed me to understand that such a network is what secures a poet's success. *Raw Heaven* was reviewed at length in the *New York Times Book Review* by J. D. McClatchy, who didn't always love it, but who *saw* it. I worked incredibly hard to be seen, to stand out. Then my next book, *Take Heart*, was reviewed by Jay Parini for the *New York Times*. My poetry was flourishing.

Phillis, carrying her books with her increasingly strained

shoulder, did everything not to be seen in person, but everything to be seen in print. She sent out her poems relentlessly. In the decade between 1989 and 1999, with her position at the University of Maryland, she was as ambitious as I was.

4.

By now, twenty-five years later, the Poetry in Motion Program has become a New York City cultural institution, a brand element of the PSA. What Elise and I thought might last a mere year has been embraced by millions. It is as deeply a part of New York as the tunnel inside bedrock that carries a subway train itself. When Elise and I, with Neil Neches from the Metropolitan Transit Authority, compiled our first anthology, it was after a harried commuter wanted to know where he could buy a Poetry in Motion placard of "The Armful," a Robert Frost poem he had seen on the subway. After a three-year-old wouldn't stop talking about "Magic Words," an Inuit poem her mother read to her while they rode the bus, her mom wanted a copy of the poem.

Elise, Neil, and I did extensive homework, looking for short poems that represented the various varied voices of poets, from the ancients right up to the present. Since citizens of the entire world ride on New York City's public transit, we tried to reflect the whole world. We looked for poems that would speak to all ethnicities, genders, ages. We looked for voices to stimulate the exhausted, inspire the frustrated, comfort the burdened, and enchant even the youngest passenger... in English and in English translations from the multitude of languages spoken in New York.

We dedicated the book to all the reader-riders who loved the poems on their routes, and said, "Now you have them for your own."[11]

5.

Moo shu pork, black bean sauce, steamed pea shoots. A fines herbes omelette with chèvre? A frisée salad? A baguette? How about a nice, chopped liver sandwich on rye with a dill pickle? Phillis and I have never dieted together. We always have full cream, full butter. We've never substituted low fat for anything—certainly not low-fat poetry.

We were realizing our roles in that Anglo-Saxon riddle for which the answer was "Ship's Figurehead," each carving ourselves into the figureheads of the sailing vessels of our lives. Phillis's first book won a prestigious poetry contest. To my complete surprise, she up and decided, after she passed her comprehensive exams, that she would not write a dissertation, rightly thinking at that time that she would be pegged as an academic. Instead, she seized her career, searched for a university position as a poet, found one, and began an eleven-year commute from New York to Maryland, a grueling enterprise that at one point would leave her with a painful condition called frozen shoulder. We had stopped being girls, as the riddle says, and began being gray queens and men, and most fearfully and electrically, we were flying with the birds (and sometimes diving under the waves and dying with the fishes).

I felt safe in my hideout at Friends Seminary, with my Saturday routine. Instead of following a job, I picked a place, New York, evolving my life there with the spiritual supervision of a therapist I think now was more of a sensei, in the manner of a Japanese guiding teacher and mentor. Much later, I learned after her illness and death, that her associates called her "The Queen." I needed a queen. I secretly thought of myself as a queen—and my model was that brilliantly styled *Reine des lettres*: Richard Howard. He led a consummate, independent literary life, didn't he? Couldn't I do that?

During this time, I had a long, passionate, but highly ritualized eleven-year affair with a European composer. He would arrive on Saturdays, after I wrote the poem, and we would spend the late afternoon, evening, and a long Sunday morning together, the light shifting around our bodies, the bed, the kitchen. He was a sensuous cook. Pumpkin agnolotti with sage butter, fried zucchini flowers. Meals punctuated by lovers' strolls around the city—and by shouting matches, slammed doors, huffy stormings away, a sink full of dirty dishes, and makeup sex.

A brilliant musician, he was called a "New Romantic." During the many concerts of New Music I attended, often bored I have to admit, I counted syllables in my head. We both were experimenting aesthetically; we both urged each other on in our careers, in our adult-size game of parallel play. But when I became pregnant, we understood that we were not prepared to be parents. He would not help me. I could not do it alone.

There are writers who feel you can have both the journey and the nest, but I am not one of them. I knew I could not also be a mother. I did not have the psychological stamina, nor did I have the means (or *would* have the means) to build the paid support system required to be a mother. I was an imaginary Jo March, an imaginary Jane Eyre, a heroine who knew she would have to work for her living. No one would give me any money. No one would launch me. If I had a child, the child would be my sole responsibility. I had no models of the man who would step in and do his share. Or a woman who was fulfilled with the idea of being a nurturing mom. At bottom, I did not want to be a mother. I had been one, or I had been supposed to be one from the age of twelve to eighteen, and the six punitive years of my daily failure at the task of being a grown woman—caring for my sister, and propping up my father, and waiting for my complicated mother, who nurtured me in so many ways, to recognize how inappropriate it was to ask me to fulfill her roles—had deformed me the way constant wind deforms a tree. I was no longer made like other people.

"I remember when you told me," Phillis said to me recently. "You used the word 'potential,' and started to cry."

What kept me from blowing to the ground and splintering? Poetry. And what would give me a leg up in the poetry world of achievement and recognition? The profound persistence that my early life engendered in me. And a self-protection that physically disabled friends seem to understand. Then, I did not see myself as part of the huge invisibly disabled world. I did not share an identity with disability. It was not part of the pull-yourself-up-by-the-bootstrap (what *were* bootstraps, anyway?) world I grew up in. But I had been de-formed, un-formed, and re-formed by carrying a burden so Sisyphean that I had a permanent kind of psychological scoliosis. I required years of psychotherapy just to feel the nurturing support that parents who anchor themselves, unlike my own parents who struggled so, and about whom I feel so tender in retrospect, give their children. And I know how complicated that syntax is. It reflects the lived life.

I had a legal abortion, but I should write, *We had a legal abortion*, for it was a mutual decision. I realize now how intimately control over my body and making space to keep using a gift for language are connected. The boundaries of language also provide boundaries for the body.

6.

I felt that a deep command of language would enable me to write what I saw so clearly in my mind. But what I saw so distinctly in my mind, after I tried to write about it, often turned out to be not what I'd felt or seen at all, but something else, something only approximating my vision. It was like feeling I could draw but not knowing how to hold a pencil. As I became more and more conscious of how I felt, I became more and more aware of the need to find ways to convey these varieties of feelings. Just as discovering hidden aspects of my life helped me to take hold of my life, discovering poetic devices, especially rhyme, helped me to take hold of my poems.

Rhyme functioned as a kind of organizer of my poetic world. Recognition of the patterns of my experience helped me to understand my life; recognition of the patterns of sound helped me to structure my experiences into art. All this is in the service of clarity, provided clarity includes rich design, for patterns "play" into one another, forming the texture of our experiences, and this playfulness forms the basis of many poetic gestures.

Once I heard a doctor say that "in the description is the prescription" and pricked up my ears because of the satisfying rhyme. I've remembered this saying because it accumulated meaning for me. I do believe that if I describe the world clearly, then I will find the order in the world, the reasons for things, or, if not the reasons, then a pattern of experience. It is this search for order that in my poems became an orderly search. Somehow, if I order *the expression*, I'll find order in the world it expresses. If I find the pattern, I'll be able to discover meaning. Also, if I have a large and worldly structure, I'll be able to say small and private things without sentimentality.

One thing, at least, that I don't fear as much is that my work will lose power by my acknowledged love of language. It's clear to me that love of language is also a love of the texture of feeling as well as thought. If the idea of formality does not polarize "language" and "life," then the poem can burst with vital incongruity as it emerges from its formal system.

My composer lover and I attempted to carry on after the abortion, the saying no that allowed us to keep making choices in our lives. But the relationship frayed.

Chapter Six:
Art of the Unspoken

1.

Our histories could have led Phillis and me to a disaster of a friendship where she was the needy one and I was the helper. It could have led us to something like my relationship to my sister. But it did not. Phillis says it's because, having no sister, she never had sister issues. But I'm not exactly sure why, except that I never believed Phillis was incompetent in the world. "What?!!" said my composer when I was leaving New York for a month in the long-ago days of snail mail, inadequate forwarding, and having to write checks in advance to pay our bills on time. "You're asking Phillis to handle your bills??? She takes an hour to put a stamp on an envelope!" It is true that ordinary responsibilities can take Phillis two or three times as long as they take me, and she is often overwhelmed. But, rolling up her long hair in a scrunchy, she always manages, excellent with anything that has to do with numbers.

I was certain that what she needed was to be trusted. (Or was it I who needed to trust?) I couldn't trust my helpless sister; my sister was a heroin addict. I did not have one hesitation about having Phillis deal with my checking account; but my sister would have wiped it out. Between Phillis and me there's a sense of intimate trust that really does feel familial. She's like a successful little sister, alive and thriving, if difficult and frustrating the way all little sisters can be. She let me push her around the way little sisters let big sisters do, but she acted secretly on her own, the way younger sisters keep secrets from older sisters, popping the big hidden info later on. Phillis did this when she got her first tenure-track academic job at the University of Maryland in 1989. I didn't even know she was applying. (Or had I, absorbed with the details of my own life, not noticed?) Suddenly, after years of being seriously considered by publishers and near misses at the Yale Series of Younger Poets, she won the University of Georgia Press First Book competition, which led to winning the 1988 Norma Farber First Book Award from the Poetry Society of America, where I had just become President. 1989 was a big year for both of us. Random House published *Take Heart*, my third book. Then both of our lives took a turn.

In 1990, Phillis magnanimously held her tongue when, during one of the times I "graduated" from therapy, I made the disastrous decision to leave the little studio on East 71st Street that I now owned and move with my composer to a large rental. After my studio apartment was free, Phillis used it temporarily, and from there she observed me begin to endure the long, difficult breakup that threw me back into psychotherapy. But at the beginning of that process, I was feeling strong as the gray queen in the Anglo-Saxon riddle. And from that initial strength—it wasn't illusory, but it was new enough so that it didn't give me endurance—I got worried about Phillis herself.

I felt her drifting. Something in her was breaking under the strain of her commute, her shoulder, and her own romantic life. I could sense her fragmenting. When we spoke, I felt I could almost pass my hand through her, she was disappearing so completely. She frightened me as I have—and would again soon—frightened myself with my own moments of disintegration, and I stepped in. Almost in the way the witness part of me watching myself making terrible mistakes could sometimes step in and grab the acting-out part of me by the shoulders, I reached out to turn Phillis in the direction of help. I suggested that she see a new therapist. My old therapist. And I pressed my therapist's number in her hand.

2.

But a mere two months later, I needed to take myself in hand. I couldn't navigate that breakup after all. My long-time, talented yet frustratingly self-absorbed lover simply refused to move out. Like Bartleby the Scrivener, he said, "I would prefer not to." Stymied and furious, I, too began to break apart, unable to direct my anger, unable to move the situation toward any sort of resolution, and I contacted my therapist.

"I'm coming back," I said imperiously, "Get rid of Phillis. We can't both see the same therapist."

"I can't do that," Joan Stein said, explaining that the therapy with Phillis had gone on too long for her consciably to stop it. She made it clear that we would have to find a way for both Phillis and me to see her. She promised to find a way for us to avoid meeting one another in terms of timing our appointments.

Shit! What had I done? Sent my little sister to our mother? Now I was sharing our mother. I didn't want to share! And yet, perhaps, I did. Joan Stein engineered exactly what she said she would. Phillis and I never bumped into one another.

And we negotiated, with surprising ease, a deal: we would never bring up our therapy with one another. Not a word would we say. Our strength would be our poetry. No couch, but a table between us. Time unfolded. We never spoke of our appointments, and certainly not of what went on in those sacred spaces. And in the following decade or so, our lives transformed. I became binational, immigrating to Canada, the birth country of my grandmother, and I married my teenage sweetheart. Phillis watched as I managed the responsibilities of my mother's illness and death, my sister's illness and death. I was a caregiver to them. Yet I did not feel I had to take care of Phillis. I watched her begin a long march toward the stability of her marriage and the next phase of her life as a poet. By 2001, she had left Maryland to become a successful full professor at Hofstra University, the editor of *The Penguin Book of the Sonnet*, and, most importantly, a Penguin poet herself with her third book, *Mercury*. Our lives thrived. Not without bumps, some serious bumps, but with an anchor: we shared a mother figure. A silent mother figure who never spoke to us about one another, and whom we never spoke of.

For two massively verbal women (and our therapist, Joan Stein, was hugely verbal, too) this would seem to be a challenge, but poetry is the art of the unspoken. Poetry, both Phillis and I are convinced, comes from preverbal experience. Its challenge is always to put the preverbal, or the nonverbal, into words that make not worldly but internal sense. That is one of the profound differences between poetry and prose.

3.

Some years later, in the trauma of our therapist's sudden stroke and the closing of her practice, we were born, so to speak, into a world where we had to mother ourselves—and we could. Or was it, having had the mothering of art retreats, the bedrock of marriages, the firmness of success with important publishers and the establishment of our own very different circles of poetry friends, as well as our firm willingness to pass on our knowledge to students, that we just plain no longer needed the help of a professional mother figure—substituting the nurturing help that a friend can lend?

Making universal art out of particular, personal trauma can easily be a cliché. But the years I spent in psychotherapy unearthed moments that were so potent I couldn't go on writing without making poems of them. How to turn self-expression into art? One solution lies in technique. In "Say You Love Me," I finally was able to tell a haunting story from my adolescence that could reverberate with universal meaning because I used a very loose terza rima, Dante's rhyme scheme in *The Divine Comedy*. Just establishing this sound system helped me lift the experience out from personal memory to living, breathing art that would connect to anyone being forced to acquiesce to a demand of love. The poem became so important to me that I read it again and again at readings, and people in audiences began to request it. Later on, when I was performing Off-Broadway in a one-woman show of poems that I wrote, *The Shimmering Verge*, this poem became the centerpiece. And it was Phillis, in talking about this poem, who said so eloquently, "The poem holds the experience, and you are no longer haunted by it." Her statement applies to any verse written from personal trauma. The experience stays alive in the lines, but the poet is no longer carrying it. This is how personal art functions. It's not poetry therapy! Real art has been shaped from what happened. The poem is not simply an expulsion of recollected emotion.

But, of course, poetry is cathartic. I confess, I don't understand how people process their experiences without making some kind of art. I know people do; they let go of emotions; they go on with their lives. But to make an art object (and I do think of poems as objects) that "holds the experience" as my friend says, so "you are no longer haunted by it" is to both have your past *and* be released by it.

Say You Love Me
by Molly Peacock

What happened earlier I'm not sure of.
Of course he was drunk, but often he was.
His face looked like a ham on a hook above

me—I was pinned to the chair because
he'd hunkered over me with arms like jaws
pried open by the chair arms. "Do you love

me?" he began to sob. "Say you love me!"
I held out. I was probably fifteen.
What had happened? Had my mother—had she

said or done something? Or had he just been
drinking too long after work? "He'll get *mean*,"
my sister hissed, "just *tell* him." I brought my knee

up to kick him, but was too scared. Nothing
could have got the words out of me then. Rage
shut me up, yet "**DO YOU?**" was beginning

to peel, as of live layers of skin, age
from age from age from him until he gazed
through hysteria as a wet baby thing

repeating, "Do you love me? Say you do,"
in baby chokes, only loud, for they came
from a man. There wouldn't be a rescue

from my mother, still at work. The same
choking sobs said, "Love me, love me," and my game
was breaking down because I couldn't do

anything, not escape into my own
refusal, *I won't, I won't,* not fantasize
a kind, rich father, not fill the narrowed zone,

empty except for confusion until the size
of my fear ballooned as I saw his eyes,
blurred, taurean—my sister screamed—unknown,

unknown to me, a voice rose and levelled
off, "I love you," I said. *"Say 'I love you,*
Dad!'" "I love you, Dad," I whispered, levelled

by defeat into a cardboard image, untrue,
unbending. I was surprised I could move
as I did to get up, but he stayed, burled

onto the chair—my monstrous fear—she screamed,
my sister, "Dad, the phone! Go answer it!"
The phone wasn't ringing, yet he seemed

to move toward it, and I ran. He had a fit—
"It's not ringing!"—but I was at the edge of it
as he collapsed into the chair and blamed

both of us at a distance. No, the phone
was not ringing. There was no world out there,
so there we remained, completely alone.

Chapter Seven:
Days & Sonnets

1.

Why should any of us be shocked when we rediscover, in age, that we are still living by decisions we made when too young to realize the outcomes? Or is it that an intuitive wisdom guided those decisions, and that is why we can continue to live by them? I write from a condominium in Toronto that I love, looking over a two-tier, flower-packed balcony garden, thinking of my ratty flat in Baltimore. When I first met Phillis, this apartment was robbed. Whoever it was took the only thing of resale value: my television. They left my manuscripts, my half of the blue china from my first marriage, and my beloved IBM variable type typewriter, a large gray land turtle of a machine, made even before the famous Selectric. It had a Garamond-like font with a beautiful, wide lower-case m. (Phillis still reminisces about how gorgeous the rounded large typeface was on the poems I submitted to the workshop.) As I sat among my prized possessions that were not robbery-worthy, I was also making a decision about my life that is still very much in effect.

Given a 24-hour day, how would I like to spend it if I could?
1. I would write.
2. I would go all out for my writing, sending out poems, applying for grants, hoping for recognition.
3. But I would not only do that, for what if I failed? What would be the substance of my life if I spent it only in chasing success? So, the very important 3 was my resolve to have a domestic day, a day of food and love and physical contact with the world. A day of noticing. Of doing my best to find the wonder in my tasks, even standing in a supermarket line noticing the way the small, slight, aged man in front of me was arranging his oranges on the conveyor belt. (There were no automated checkouts then.)
4. If all my efforts to publish my poems and have them received in the world failed, I would revel in the fact of my day. I would understand that I could not have it all. I could be a poet, or I could throw myself into a career and a family. I could not be both. Which leads me to
5. I would rely on my talent to seek and discover the people in this world with whom I could bond.

2.

When Michael Groden, my boyfriend from high school, re-appeared in my life after *Raw Heaven* was reviewed in the *New York Times Book Review* (Mike had read that review), we began an adult friendship that developed into adult love. I felt that having *the day*, which also meant not having it *all*, was essential. I was struggling financially—even though I was volunteering as President of the Poetry Society of America, helping to put poetry on the New York subways and buses, and would soon publish another book of poems.

When I began commuting to London, Ontario from New York City, for love, I surprised myself, my therapist, my students, and all my friends except Phillis by getting married to a James Joyce scholar and melanoma survivor. Phillis had predicted our marriage! When Mike and I were contemplating a trip to Nova Scotia together (ah, the travel test, that's where you *really* discover if you're in sync with somebody...) she recalls that I said to her, "I can trust him to make the reservations." Knowing how hard and how long I struggled for that kind of trust, she said, "You're going to marry this man."

Then I left the center of the North American poetry universe for the land of my paternal grandmother and her settler ancestors, finding in the harsh light and winter freeze and hardy liberalism and polite insularity an aspect of my personality and heritage that also nurtured me. In London, Ontario, on the lands of the Anishinaabek and the Haudenosaunee, there was a financial anchor and a warm bed in a house with a garden. There was time not only to write poetry, but prose, and time to paint and draw a bit, too, and people who did not seem to be endlessly striving but living their days.

I leapt.

But I took all of my New York life with me. That included my therapist, now on the phone, and that included Phillis, with whom I still had dinner in New York and who visited me, and with whom I still exchanged poems, now by fax. The tech had changed. The distance had changed. But the exchange had not changed. While Phillis was in Slovenia in 1995 on a Fulbright Fellowship; while Phillis exhausted herself job hunting; while Phillis had her Fellowship in Rome; while I sat down in London, Ontario and wrote a memoir about my choice to be childfree for which I would be paid a life-changing amount of money as an advance; while Phillis seemed to be rootless; and while I seemed to be re-rooting; we continued.

I came to my marriage with all sorts of baggage that my husband, who had known me since we were thirteen, long understood. My friendship with Phillis, and the time it took, was part of who I was. He'd have to endure the dinner-interrupting phone calls. He'd have to tolerate the 11 p.m. phone poetry priority just as he was settling in for his eight-hour sleep. He accepted the Phillis poetry disruptions. He grumbled, but he did.

And Phillis recognized that my life had profoundly changed. Just as I would have to acknowledge the transformations in her life.

3.

By the time I was fifty-four, I'd been married to Mike Groden for seven years. My parents and sister had passed away. I was released from my complex ties to them into the loving stability of a marriage that I was surprised I was capable of, to a man I let tease me. "Reading your favorite author?" he quipped as he passed me in the couch reading one of my own books—and I laughed till the cats sprang away in alarm.

4.

What was I going to do with all my formalist interests in Canada? When I met Sandy Shreve and Kate Braid in British Columbia, on a book tour for the Canadian edition of *How to Read a Poem,* I realized that there was a special brand of Canadian formal technique in poetry. Shreve and Braid, like Annie Finch in the United States, were dedicated to unearthing formally-inspired poems, and I had many discussions with Sandy that led to some thoughts about routines. Routines were what Mike and I established in our marriage, patterns that allowed us to work and live in small physical spaces while we roamed intellectually in the solitary, wide mental plains that those routines left us to.

Habit. Habits are the means by which we achieve our fate—and by which a poem fulfills its inspiration. Just the way you almost cannot believe that breakfast, lunch, dinner and eight hours of sleep will eventually energize a person to cultivate an entire life's work, it is hard to credit that the simple counting of stresses or the almost child-like capturing of rhymes will help an evanescent inspiration flower. But inside inspiration a musical regime flows and, like three square meals and a night's rest, it makes for a marvelously flexible, healthy poem.

A poem comes into being as it is built—or, to be more organic about it, as it is grown. The poem's structure develops inside its words even as the words grow the poem, the way a bud grows inside a stem.

Fences train vines. Does form *train* a poem? The way my trainer at the gym urges reps for fitness? There *are* gymnastics in traditional form. And like virtuosity in anything, basketball or piano solos, formal dexterity is built on routines. The imagination leaps because the poet urges it again and again. These leaps themselves become rhythmic.

Form does something else vigorously physical: it compresses. Because you have to meet a limit—a line length, a number of syllables, a rhyme—you have to stretch or curl a thought to meet that requirement. Curiously, as the lyrical mind works to answer that demand, the unconscious is freed to experience its most playful and most dangerous feelings. Form is safety, the safe place in which we can be most volatile.

Emily Dickinson famously wrote, "After great pain, a formal feeling comes—"[12] and technique is a great comfort, perhaps even an antidote to pain as her title suggests. I think of a story the psychoanalyst poet Frederick Feirstein once told me, how, when undergoing an excruciating medical procedure as a child, he would count sequences of five on his fingers till it was over. That count is iambic pentameter or the heartbeat line, *lubdub, lubdub*. It's no accident that we think of form as structuring the body of a poem, or that we think of poems as *having* bodies.

And formal bodies are fun. The enchanting idea that human beings are not so much defined by knowing as by *playing* comes to us by way of Johan Huizinga, the Dutch philosopher, a thinker now embraced by game theorists. Huizinga said in *Homo Ludens* that "All poetry is born of play... the nimble play of wit and readiness." But to be truly ready, we must rehearse. Musicians rehearse to perform, as do dancers. Athletes of all stripes practice to be ready for the interplay of rules and inspiration. Form is the beauty of play. What is beauty, by the way? Let's say it is the sudden encounter between unlikely entities—like "fun" and "regimen." For me, the beauty of form is the sudden union of boomerangingly free inspiration with disciplined language.

Difficulty and discipline scare some people. But they excite poets who tackle formal patterns. I am always trying to get others to read more poetry, and when I find myself saying to reluctant readers, "It's not really that difficult," I half wince. I might try to deliver poetry as simple, but I know that a formal poem is as satisfyingly complex as an illuminated page from the Book of Kells. To go back to sports: a great game stunningly played can be breathtakingly complicated. Or think of cuisine: it's exciting to try to sort out the layers of spices in a mouthful of something a dazzlingly experienced cook has constructed. The human activity of making *enjoys* these complications. Not when you start out, of course; then you need simple instructions, a recipe, and formalists adore providing those, too.

By the time Braid and Shreve put together the second edition of their anthology *In Fine Form*, Canadian poets happily found that they no longer had to apologize—much less justi-fy—the use of form in poetry. There are twenty-first-century sonnets, triolets, villanelles, and roundelays so colloquial they are transparent to the naked eye of the ordinary reader. No longer is free verse fiercely contrasted to form. All who prac-tice, or experiment with, the defined repetitions that are the playground of poetry remind us that no poem exists without its shape and sound. Intrigued by the varieties of form and seduced by the paradox of the liberation from constraints *by constraints* (patterns do seem to liberate thoughts we've kept hidden from ourselves), most poets have stopped thinking about formal poetry as jail. Why think of a formal apparatus as exterior bars for containment? Form is an inside.

Because contemplation and emotion are interior, we can think of their means of expression, poetry, as the inside of an inside.[13]

5.

One of the intersections of poetry and friendship that Phillis and I have concerns the sonnet. Phillis has written the odd sonnet, but they are a pillar of my poetic life. Yet I don't know nearly what Phillis knows about that verse form. She understands the sonnet historically and comprehensively, having compiled, with her own genius for selection, *The Penguin Book of the Sonnet*—a publication that has already lasted more than two decades. As I was initiating Poetry in Motion with Elise Paschen, Phillis was working on this mag-num opus of an anthology, and writing, with both trepida-tion and elegance, an extensive introduction to the sonnet in English.

I watched and read as this work of a poet's scholarship emerged, and nervously hoped for the best when Phillis had to make all the edits from Italy in the days before email attachments, calling and faxing North America. I was nervous for her because she often suffers extreme anxiety when she writes discursive prose of any kind. But if you read her prose, you'd never know that.

Levin's critical voice (yes, I'm returning to the professional Levin here) is so erudite, and her perceptions so inclusive, that it's time for her to speak for herself. Here are the first seven paragraphs of the introduction. The first paragraph I almost memorized, having seen it in iteration after iteration. In these paragraphs, she instigates a conversation with the sonnet, touching on so many of the themes of our conversations over time: rooms, architecture, play, dialectic, the volta (or turn), and the imagery of a pond. (Phillis and I are not ocean people. Our preferred bodies of water are streams and lakes or a pond set like an opal in greenery.) Here's Levin.

FROM INTRODUCTION
THE PENGUIN BOOK OF THE SONNET
Phillis Levin

The sonnet is a monument of praise, a field of play, a chamber of sudden change. In its limited space it has logged, from the start, the awakening of a rational being to an overwhelming force in the self or the world. Its legacy of fourteen lines offers myriad challenges and opportunities, ranging from the technical to the spiritual. As a highly focused form, the sonnet attracts contradictory artistic impulses: in choosing and succumbing to the form, the poet agrees to follow the rules of the sonnet, but that willing surrender releases creative energy. The earliest sonnets record the unceasing conflict between the law of reason and the law of love, the need to solve a problem that cannot be resolved by an act of will, yet finds its fulfillment, if not its solution, only in the poem. Thematically and structurally, this tension plays itself out in the relationship between a fixed formal pattern and the endless flow of feeling. The poet experiences the illusion of control and the illusion of freedom, and from the meeting of those illusions creates the reality of the poem.

What makes the sonnet so compelling for both reader and writer? Not only is it one of the only poetic forms with a predetermined length and a specific—though flexible—set of possibilities for arranging patterns of meaning and sound, but it is also a blueprint for building a structure that remains open to the unknown, ready to lodge an unexpected guest. The sonnet inscribes in its form an instruction manual for its own creation and interpretation: it is a portrait of the mind in action, a miniguide to the progress of an emotion that tells us when to anticipate an irreversible turn. People are drawn to watching an Olympic athlete going through a certain set of motions known in advance, but executed differently each time. The same moves are never performed by one person exactly the same way each time, and the difference between the performances of two individuals can be dramatic. But when it comes to poetry, people are often surprised to discover the extraordinary range of difference in the treatment of a particular form. As with any established pattern—from figure skating to break dancing—the results can be tedious or sublime.

The easiest thing to say about a sonnet is that it is a fourteen-line poem with a particular rhyme scheme and a particular mode of organizing and amplifying patterns of image and thought; and that, if written in English, the meter of each line usually will be iambic pentameter. Taken as a whole, these fourteen lines compose a single stanza, called a quatorzain, the name given to any fourteen-line form. But though a sonnet typically has fourteen lines, fourteen lines do not guarantee a sonnet: it is the behavior of those lines in relation to each other—their choreography—that identifies the form. There are two basic types of sonnets, the Italian (Petrarchan) and the English (Shakespearean); at least that is what we say in retrospect. In truth, by the time Petrarch and Shakespeare met the sonnet, each in his own era, its form was already prevalent, an excessively imitated fashion. Their names are thereby associated with specific patterns that they perfected but did not themselves invent. But each poet brought the sonnet to its peak in his own native language, in terms of consolidating its structural integrity and affirming its expressive power.

In Italian, the word *stanza* means "room." It may help to conceptualize the sonnet as a room (or stage) that can be divided in a number of different ways to serve many functions. Since its overall dimensions and circumference do not change, whatever occurs within that space will always be determined to some degree by its size and haunted by the presence of its former occupants. Even if we rearrange, replace, or remove some of the furniture, the marks will still be there to remind us of how things were positioned in the past. The English sonnet, whose mode of organization differs greatly from the Italian form that gave birth to it, still carries the trace of its ancestry—not only in the number of lines determining the form, but also in the place where the Italian sonnet registers a change that can feel seismic in so small a space.

In any language, the sonnet has an undeniably recognizable shape, easy to see at a distance. This visual impression results not only from its fourteen lines, but also from the average number of syllables per line, which is also quite consistent, and varies only by a syllable or two from one language to another. Each line's metrical structure affects how long it takes to say the line and with how much breath, and to some degree how much space (as well as time) the line occupies. Nonetheless, this predetermined length—its most obvious, superficial characteristic—is not its most important quality. Sometimes the sonnet looks like a little rectangular box ("I am a little world made cunningly," Donne says); sometimes we see a bipartite structure with a white space, a gap, separating the first eight lines (the octave) from the second six (the sestet). Sometimes we see a form subdivided into two quatrains or four-line units, followed by two tercets (units of three lines); or we see a series of three quatrains, and then a single couplet (two lines) standing alone. But the quintessential feature of its design is not as apparent. Whatever its outward appearance, by virtue of its infrastructure the sonnet is asymmetrical. The dynamic property of its structure depends on an uneven distribution of lines, of the weight they carry. It is top-heavy, fundamentally. Opposition resides in its form the way load and support contend in a great building.

Being dialectical, the sonnet is divided by nature: its patterns of division multiply perspective and meaning. But that does not mean the eye will always find the dividing point. We may locate these divisions sonically, by noting the arrangement of lines into units that follow a particular rhyme scheme. Though the variety of rhyme schemes is limited, the possibilities are surprisingly varied. And the arrangement of lines into patterns of sound serves a function we could call architectural, for these various acoustical partitions accentuate the element that gives the sonnet its unique force and character: the *volta*, the "turn" that introduces into the poem a possibility for transformation, like a moment of grace.

The *volta*, the sonnet's turn, promotes innovative approaches because whatever has occurred thus far, a poet is compelled, by inhabiting the form, to make a sudden leap at a particular point, to move into another part of the terrain. Reading sonnets, one constantly confronts the infinite variety of moves a poet can make to negotiate a "turn." Though a poet will sometimes seem to ignore the *volta*, its absence can take on meaning, as well—that is, if the poem already feels like a sonnet. We could say that for the sonnet, the *volta* is the seat of its soul. And the reader's experience of this turn (like a key change) reconfigures the experience of all the lines that both precede and follow it. The *volta* foregrounds the paradigm, making us particularly conscious of the rhyme scheme; likewise, the poet's anticipation of the *volta* guides every move he or she will make. The moment a pebble is dropped into a pond, evidence of that action resonates outward, and at the same time continues to draw the eye back to the point from which all succeeding motions ensue.[14]

6.

My soul receives its sustenance in American poetry, so I was at sea when I first emigrated from the United States to Canada. I would open an anthology of Canadian poets and barely recognize any names at all. As I read increasingly, I found poetry with different designs from the American works I was used to. My reading provoked another project, this one undertaken at first with adventurous and stylish Halli Villegas who began Tightrope Books, then with savvy Jim Nason, and last with serenely energetic Anita Lahey and Biblioasis. Throughout, a smart managing editor, Heather Wood, kept us going. *The Best Canadian Poetry in English* began in 2008, the first anthology of its kind in Canada. We hoped to publish an annual of the most compelling and vigorous poems published in Canada's literary journals from the previous year, and, like Poetry in Motion on New York's subways and buses, it's going strong.

From sound poems to confessional poems, from loose-limbed narratives to formal verse, from bellows to whispers, from the urban landscape to the arctic, from west to east and all directions in between, prosodic decisions, geographical propensities and cultural proclivities give Canadian poetry its astonishing variety and its labyrinthine nature. From the patterns of Indigenous voices to plainspoken settler vocabulary to the linguistic zest of immigrant voices, *The Best Canadian Poetry in English* addresses all.

Literary magazines are often the first places a poet publishes, usually long before a poet collects the work into book form. For this reason, editors of literary magazines take on the role of literary explorers, searching out and discovering the vibrant and new among poets. For *The Best Canadian Poetry in English* series, we reviewed as many issues of literary journals from the previous year as possible. Because I did not believe that a committee, with all its compromises, could select whatever one, with trepidation, could consider the best poems, each year I picked a single poet-editor to choose among the chosen for the volume. I hoped by these changes to reflect the aesthetic vigor, and the wild diversity in inclination and taste among Canadian poets—or maybe I should say among Canadian poetries...

I had to take on the challenge of defining a Canadian poem, even though I don't really believe that a single poem of any kind can represent a nation. So here are a few thoughts about what a Canadian poem can enact:

It seems to me that it is a poem that takes its time but does not lose its intensity. One that wanders but is not afraid of getting lost, a poem that is willing to stumble because it takes on rough or unknown emotional or intellectual terrain, but rights itself again, a poem that admits a reader as a companion, a worthy witness to experience, whether that experience is a heady, brainy one, or a quiet, domestic few minutes. That the poem proceeds in time without losing intensity means that each one is forged of passion and also heated with a virtuosity of craft...

What I began to see, from poets from diverse backgrounds, provinces, ages and personal categories, is a unity, a core, something identifiable as a gesture in Canadian poetry itself, not in the poets' backgrounds or personalities, but in the poems they produce, poems that presume a kind of companionship with their readers and assume their readers' willingness to undertake a tandem adventure. They are not poems that stand apart from an audience, inviting the audience to watch them, and in this they are distinct from many of their American and British and Australian counterparts. Instead, these poems often fully enter the imaginative ground where writer and reader are one.

I see a companionship of poet and reader, the invitation of a welcoming host rather than the dazzle of the showoff.[15]

Chapter Eight
Cazenovia Idyll

1.

"Are we living our lives," my husband asked me in 2011, "or administering them?" We were sitting with a calendar trying to figure out our commitments in three countries with careers at full tilt, his illness, our many students to manage, as well as my new life as a biographer. I was determined for a creative solution to emerge. Whenever I get to the place of pushing to find a solution, I know even as I push so hard, that it will only come when I am relaxed. Yet I only relax when forced to relax! Two things could do this for me: getting a terrible cold or the sheer insistence of my husband. Lying in bed with him would lend me a sense of calm that I could not experience on my own. There is a parenting aspect to marriage, and even as I was the intermittent caregiver for his many years living with cancer, he was a caregiver for me, absolutely insisting that we get into bed at a certain, regular hour. Resolutely rising to an alarm clock. Together we crossed off some of the travel on our calendars, some of the lecturing and some of the teaching, giving our schedule a haircut. But this amounted to a kind of efficient administration. It didn't quite return me to what I think of as *living*.

Despite his alarm setting, I usually rose on my own inner clock. Leaving him asleep, I crept to the kitchen early every Saturday morning to write the poem that would connect me to the center of the wilderness inside me, something rhythmical and pulsing, something almost mitochondrially ancient. Yet grabbing those few hours was not enough to preserve a talent that I was born with, but that the world constantly worked to take away. To have a gift for something that is not understood or valued in the greater world, for something that is discounted, not an obvious part of an economy, mystifying to businessmen, held suspect by politicians, viewed as a hobby when in fact it beats at the core of life, forces the person with that gift always to engage in wily espionage to protect and nurture it. Sometimes it's an outright battle, and it requires a warrior's strategizing. I had to figure out a way to reclaim time for poetry, the thing that would keep me in touch not only with what made me human, but with what made me part of a greater universe.

So, one morning when I'd stopped looking for solutions to these dilemmas, an answer came to me. What if I recreated those artist's retreats that had so nurtured my poetry when younger? What if I took those principles and applied them to a place, if I could find that place, where I could restore? During our many drives between Ontario and New York, Mike and I had located a town that was as close to a New England town in upstate New York as one could find. Because my husband and I traveled with cats, we were always searching for a place that would accept them, or one with a layout that would allow us to sneak them in. Cazenovia, New York—a wealthy town on the lands of the Haudenosaunee, full of the summer homes of former nineteenth- and early twentieth-century robber barons including Standard Oil financier Benjamin Brewster—had three such inns. One of them, in Brewster's former summer home, was located directly on Cazenovia Lake, with a view of the water, rooms on three floors, and a restaurant, too.

I proposed to Phillis that we spend a week in Cazenovia together, and she was on to try our poet's retreat *à deux*. It took time, especially after the first year, when we began to stretch it to ten days in the next year and the next. For nine summers we traveled to what the residents simply call Caz. Our husbands groused. But we were going; we were spending. I was renting my car; Phillis, who doesn't drive, was hiring a car service; and we were planning. We needed cars to lug all those books and drafts. After the first year proved so profoundly nourishing and productive, in following years we'd start thinking about it the winter beforehand. Preparing our visit was like preparing to paint a room. We'd spend months as if with mental masking tape, drawing off the lines for the future fresh paint. We'd both arrive armed with drafts, the bits and pieces accumulated through the year that we either didn't have time to develop or didn't know how to build up or couldn't concentrate on. I'd keep a box in my little office where I put those folders, holding Cazenovia in my mind like a romance. Tracking down these almost abandoned fragments of writing through the months beforehand altered our focus, derailed the trains of our obligations, let our minds disperse into a creative cloud. By the time July arrived, our boxes, our portable printers, our reams of paper, our books, my purple pads, and our little presents for each other were packed in the cars.

Two poets on vacation in a robber baron's former summer house? I can't separate the atmosphere of privilege from the history of the two girls whose lust for language wound them around the wounds of family dysfunction and societal dismissal to grow into an adulthood with an absolute insistence that poetry is life.

For us, poetry is a practical necessity, like the stoves, refrigerators, and cars we depend on, a cultural necessity like taxes, marriage certificates, and cemetery plots. Poetry is a roof over our heads, constructed by the two-by-fours of contemporary middle-class North American existence. It took a certain amount of money to fund our retreat in a world that denies the necessity of creativity. And a certain amount of self-worth to insist on it. In the Obama years, before Donald Trump was elected, before the #MeToo movement, before George Floyd was murdered, before white feminists acknowledged their whiteness, Phillis and I each had a modestly priced Virginia Woolfian room of our own in a former mansion on a lake of gorgeous sunsets that, in a global environmental crisis, was dying of algae blooms.

Within these massive cultural and moral contradictions, all mixed up with finding a way to write, a post-menopausal poet and her poet friend became summer fixtures at the Brewster Inn for ten days a year for nearly a decade. The nine summers rescued us from a devastating series of personal losses. In 2012, we began losing our mentors: Elfie Raymond, Phillis's beloved philosophy professor at Sarah Lawrence, and Joan Stein. My dear older friend's husband died, and after that, she cut off from me. Then there were more and more frequent cancer recurrences for my husband. By the end of the nine years, after a roller coaster of a drug trial, Mike was dying. Phillis's father was seriously ill, then passed away. Her mother became increasingly frail and died. Half a year later came the pandemic. It's said that the only subjects of lyric poetry are love and death. Love and death are the reasons that we spent nine culturally changing, increasingly environmentally challenging summers in Cazenovia.

There we wrote.

Desks were left in the two poets' rooms. It took us a couple of days to settle into our routine. I think of this as a couple of days to let sediment sink down deep into the lake floor of the unconscious. For each of us to uncurl. In the first couple of years, it passed through my mind that we could invite others, that it really could be a group artists' retreat. No! No big arrangements, no administering, no distractions. It was a Herculean effort to explain to friends who lived nearby that we were not getting together with them.

We kept a mutual diary for all of these summers, and we followed a routine. We'd meet on the second-floor landing around 7:30 a.m. and walk into town, crossing a highway where, even though there was a traffic light, we always felt a pedestrian could be killed. We ate at a diner called Emma's: a huge breakfast of poached eggs and pancakes and fruit for me, and for Phillis, a Western omelet with hot sauce and rye toast. We shared the fruit. We sat in our booth with the huge fans going—no air conditioning. After a few years, no one bothered to look up and stare the way the men in overalls sitting at the counter stared at first. Soon we were simply the poets who came every year. We'd call another little restaurant to order our lunches, and then walk down the street of the historic town to pick them up. Then we'd cross a street and veer off into the grass paths of a willow preserve. The grass was still dewy, and sometimes we'd interrupt a rabbit. We'd walk in silence by the grasses and up onto the abandoned towpath past a pond with its basso profundo of frogs, alive in a green haiku.

And then the highway. The semis barreling down. The crossing that took our lives in our hands. At last, the driveway of the Brewster and up the steps to get hot water for my extra tea and Phillis's coffee, then saying goodbye at the staircase, and agreeing when we would meet at the end of the day. We would be settled in our rooms by 10:30 a.m.—and we wouldn't emerge till 7 p.m.

The Brewster Inn was like one of our restaurant meetings writ large, the table becoming a three-story inn with a staircase to our brain-lairs. After we disappeared into our rooms, I don't know what Phillis did all day. ("I was writing poetry!"

she reminded me, both quizzically and indignantly.) I thought about the poem and napped, made changes, ate my lunch in tiny bits for hours, and resented every email I had to respond to, every outside interference, then changed my clothes and went to the local swimming hole at the end of the day. After that was the rush to dinner, getting what I was working on printed in the version that was ready for Phillis. This was the emerging stage for the poem. We were our first publics, a way-station from the deep unconscious state to the finished thing.

We met in the line for dinner. Line? Oh yes, the restaurant at this inn is very popular. And the covered patio much in demand. Whatever we wore, we never blended in with the martini-drinking coiffed individuals who are the usual customers of the Brewster, the well-to-do locals who can afford it. And of course, Phillis and I had our table preference. Because we were very particular. We needed a certain angle on the water. We are sunset watchers. We needed a certain waitperson. We needed our perfection and our attention because we were not casual about this. We were safeguarding the mental energy it takes to write our poems in a world that both rewarded us for the products we produced but that refused to make a space for the production. We had ten perfect, ritualized nights, including our walk to the dock, our choosing of what we were going to eat: Shrimp cocktail! Crabcakes. Wedge salad. Beet salad. Maple salmon. Chantilly potatoes. Rhubarb pie. Homemade strawberry ice cream. We thrilled to the thunderstorm or wind that drove everyone inside but us. Our exclamations about the sky. The clouds. The line of the water as it disappeared into the horizon. And, we had our conversation.

It took about three days of discussing practicalities before we'd sink, deep, into the stories of our families, and surface our feelings and discoveries. This is about how long it took us to get deep into the poems (and for me sometimes the prose) we were writing. After three days, we could slip through a mirror into the world on the other side, the world that as children we felt somehow had to be there, just as in the fairy tales where the person would disappear through the silvered glass into a reflected spot that was both the world and not the world. We'd entered the queendom of metaphor.

After we ate, the typescripts would come out and we would read. Old-style. On paper. And we would respond with our usual, our natural enthusiasm. Where was our judgment? Mixing with caution and wonder. If we had something to offer each other, there, in our sixties, it was a wealth of shared technical expertise and a respect for, what shall I call it? Emergence. For watching something emerge, as a gardener comes to the same garden every day noticing something else emerging. And we enjoy—revere?—what is blossoming. We are proof of growth in age. This time together was a marker. And so our conversation might have been about a semi-colon. Or about a vision or a dream. We wrote down our suggestions with our fountain pens or our mechanical pencils, and we took each other's suggestions, or we didn't. But we didn't resist.

When I sense resistance from Phillis, I know I'm pressing something and should stop. You don't touch a budding flower. You can knock the bud off that way. You have to get close but leave it to itself.

When everyone left the restaurant, and, as usual, we were shutting the place down, at last we would have to move. Then we'd walk to the dock, or occasionally venture across that treacherous highway to go listen in the dark to the bullfrogs at the pond. At last, we'd go up the coffered staircase to the second-floor landing; then I'd ascend another flight to my room with its green lamp in the shape of a ceramic rabbit on the chest of drawers, and leave that lamp on, with no other light, and call my husband. No matter where Mike and I were for the three decades of our marriage, we called each other at night. We had a desultory conversation, because I was tired of talking, but he was alone, so he needed to talk, and I listened, and then I got into my nightgown and lay in bed, watching a little TV, then flipping it off, and listening to the rain, or the late-shift voices in the restaurant kitchen. And sleeping.

2.

Let me stop and speak further about our psychological interiors, and how palliative Cazenovia was for both of us. But in order to explain, let me backtrack to New York, to the time after Joan Stein had her stroke, and after her colleague called us, saying, "She will never practice again," when Phillis and I were jolted into a profound new reality. Phillis and I met at a new iteration of the old Café des Artistes, the Leopard at des Artists, at 1 West 67th in March, 2012, to eat and remember and find our way through the shock. I was crying copiously. The grief I felt had the purity of a child's emotions: it wasn't marbled with multiple overlays the way adult loss can be. It was just abject loss, worthy of complete, immediate, and voluminous tears. I should have brought an entire box of Scotties to the restaurant, I cried so hard. And Phillis had tears in her eyes.

It was a late lunch time at the Leopard, with Howard Chandler Christy's 1930s murals of naked girls. Hardly anyone else was there. Phillis and I sat there as sisters, mourning a mother figure under whose eye, the eye that really saw us, that beamed a healing understanding on us, we'd grown. Joan was the sun to two cotyledons who had become remarkably sturdy, substantial plants. I don't know if Phillis actually held my hand, but I recall her as holding my hand when we looked at the menu ordering a meal neither of us found spectacular. It was cardboard in the midst of the false sensuality of the naked lady murals. But strangely appropriate, since we were spiritually naked and alone.

Four months later, exhausted emotionally, I crept to Cazenovia and asked Phillis if we could switch rooms. Until I found my beloved (and cheaper) room with the ceramic rabbit lamp, Phillis and I preferred a certain lake view room and agreed that each of us could reserve it every other year. It was Phillis's turn for that room. But I was such a wreck, I asked if I could have it again. And Phillis gave it to me. I proceeded to spend hours of many days prone on a yoga mat in restorative poses, just to be able to function.

The poems I wrote at this time let me consider what is truly essential in life. Is there an essence of a person? Something that cannot be changed no matter what? And is that spiritual? Physical? Something in the medulla oblongata? Some vibe of the vagus nerve? Phillis and her then new husband Jack visited Joan, but they (perhaps more sensibly than I) limited their contact with her. Joan was changed. She was no longer Phillis's therapist. And in some ways the flowering of their relationship had been celebrated: Phillis married Jack. Their romance matured, and their miracle continued.

But my enterprise in therapy, always supported by my late husband, who believed in psychological quests—and was on one himself—was to understand what the core of a self is. Joan and I had an ongoing dialog about this because I met her at age twenty-six, when I felt I had no core. I was deciding to be a poet; I was deciding to leave my first husband; I was feeling who I was. And Joan, despite her stroke and huge memory loss, remembered me. Once she had reached out to me as the acrobat's receiver hands are ready to catch the flying acrobat. And now it was my turn to be the receiver. Joan flew into my hands, and we began what I now feel is the amazing coda of our twenty-eight-year conversation: a post-therapeutic relationship defining new ways of being with one another, our essences meeting in new ways.

MANDALA IN THE MAKING
at the Asia Society
by Molly Peacock

Three Tibetan monks make a sand painting
(under spotlights) in a reverential hush,
the circular world before them everything:

a cosmos, a brain, a divine palace lush
with lotuses and pagodas in children's
paintbox colors. "Excuse me, my friend is

recovering from an accident. She's a ...
painter. May we ask you some questions?"
(Have I introduced *you,* my former analyst,

as my painter-*friend*?) You point with your cane
to the mandala-in-sand and ask, "*Three*
artists? How do they decide who does what?"

"He's the boss!" One monk points to the other.
The boss beams above the bowls and brass funnel
he wields like a wand. When they're done,

they'll brush it all away. You can't believe it.
Nothing stays, (including the memory you've lost).
What lasts? The pattern the monks have

memorized. Their burnt-down temple returns as this circular core.
                              Only when
something's over can its shape materialize.

"Mandala in the Making" is the last poem in the book that grew from my new, post-therapeutic interactions with Joan, *The Analyst: Poems*. And it isn't until the last two lines that the poem—and that I, the poet—understood the shape of our relationship. Time turned into space in this poem. A stroke that altered a woman did not alter some essential core of her, a core I related to; I did not back away. After three quarters of a century on earth, I realize that one of my most positive qualities is being willing to face things. Not to run away. To step up. Quaking. But to meet whatever it is, even a volcano, standing on two feet the way I met my father in his rages. Once, on a National Endowment for the Arts Committee in the United States, I signed on as being willing to testify to a hostile Congress to the value of the poems I voted for. Staying with it, lasting, standing up and saying why, it's spiritual to me. Even standing up for an aesthetic choice has a spiritual essence. So, I decided to stand up for Joan.

I looked for small museums to take Joan to, and the Asia Society in Manhattan was perfect. The situation in the poem is exactly as it was. I took her to see the phenomenon of Buddhist sand painting. I, who believe in preservation, conservation, archives, libraries, diaries, dried flower albums, safety deposit boxes, fireproof storage units, legacies, and houses on stilts, can barely grasp the idea of purposely destroying a work of art. It puts me in agony. Yet the destruction of the artwork allows for the growth of realization. I had to use three-line stanzas, just as Phillis would deploy in her poem, "An Anthology of Rain." Even without the Christian overlay of a trinity (an overlay I don't mind at all), the tercet is the most spiritual of stanza structures. It is inherently as graceful and stable as a geometric triangle.

I use the first six stanzas to explain the situation. Then, I am able to answer the question I pose: What lasts? It is pattern. That is why a formal approach in poetry is so essential for me. Repetition, and the realizations that come with re-peated action (even repeated mistakes where we say in ex-asperation, "Again?????") create the richness of life, and the reason to live, and even how to live. The middle line of the last stanza of "Mandala in the Making" breaks in two, to compose a dropped stanza.

> turns as this circular core.
>   Only when

Losses are breaks in a continuing reality, so of course the last stanza is different from the others. Finally in the last line and a half I understand something: Time funnels back into Space. Only when time stops do we understand its events. "Only when something's over can its shape materialize." "Materialize" rhymes with "memorize" hidden at the begin-ning of the stanza. So often solutions remain hidden until, irrepressibly, they spring from bewildered considerations.

Phillis and I talked about how a dropped stanza functions, and this led to our thinking about how knowledge emerges in dialectic. "Neither of us alone arrives at the solution," she reminded me. "We are each trying to solve a problem, and would each come to [our own] solution, but together we come to a unique and more magical solution—through dialectic."

3.

Phillis, in 1995, after settling in Ljubljana, Slovenia, wrote a poem called "Table Manners." It is in the form of an in-terview, and it, too, finds its solution suddenly in the last two lines. Although "Table Manners" and "Mandala in the Making" are different in strategy, the discovery in the last lines of the poem is similar. The poem wonderfully fits into our pattern of eating and talking. And the first question is the tipoff to the last two lines, though by the time we get to the end of the poem, we don't remember this initial query, the profoundest interrogation: "What do you need?" Each piece of tableware, the essential cutlery of knife, fork, and spoon, the beauty of the fork and the mirror of the spoon, proceed in stately order through the smearing of honey, eating of melon, sipping of soup, as in a gently formal meal, until necessity re-enters the poem at the end. And the answer to "What do you need?" comes around to just about nothing. It is shocking because the tableware indicates a richness of environment, and the answer is so ascetic that all the sensuality of honey, melon, and soup is reduced to: "I can do without it, I can do without/ almost anything, if necessary."

TABLE MANNERS
by Phillis Levin

What do you need?

    A knife, a fork, a spoon.

Is the order important?

    For my purposes, yes.

Say more about this, please.

    The knife, first. A knife does more
    than the rest.

Do you mean when it comes to eating?

    Yes. It can cut, it can spear,
    it can smear honey, as well as do damage.

Why a fork, then?

> It is the most beautiful of the three:
> the curve of its tines, especially,
> and the way it rests in the hand.

And the spoon, what about the spoon?

> Not so important, unless one is a child—
> though for soup there is really no choice,
> unless one resorts to nothing at all.

Don't you need it for anything else?

> Melons, maybe. And the mirror
> a spoon can be, or the image of love in repose.

But it isn't necessary.

> I can do without it, I can do without
> almost anything, if necessary.

The kind of emotional and psychological deprivation Phillis experienced as a child reappears in those lines created by Levin. Levin's lines end a poem of interrogation. What moves me is the determination. One of Phillis's best personal qualities is determination. She does not deviate from her task; she goes forward—aslant, perhaps, but forward. In the spoon's mirror is "an image of love in repose." To me, that is Phillis and Jack, an acceptance of lasting love. Yet after the image of love in repose comes the line "But it isn't necessary." Yes, earlier in life, Phillis had learned to do without in order to survive. Yet poetry itself supplies needs as Levin demonstrates in "Table Manners." She shows how manners create a manner of survival. Manners can be seen to cover up a raw need, such as the need that comes from learning to live, emotionally, on almost nothing. But her life experience (and therapy) gave Phillis the idea that she could have something that lasted. Even though the speaker in Levin's poem can survive in a state of desolation, the Phillis I know embraced her life, and that is the love reflected in the spoon.

Chapter Nine:
An Elsewhere That Is Home

1.

The reflection of love is in our diary entries from these years. At odd moments at breakfast in Cazenovia, together we made a shorthand of weather, food, and poem titles. We started them in 2011 in little notebooks, which I would take home, elaborately xerox, and send to Phillis. I was the one who suggested the brief diaries and took charge of them because I felt Phillis would never get around to copying them for me and I wanted these records. After all, I'm a biographer as well as a poet. Stuff like this is important to me. That's why I despaired when I lost (no doubt deeply misfiled) our first notebook. Phillis insists that she has the copy I made for her, but it is buried in the numerous boxes of papers she keeps, and she is always in some sort of minor domestic upheaval that prevents her from looking for it. I haven't insisted. Yet I would love to read that very first entry. Re-reading the notebooks, I see they are often quite ordinary little notes of weather, food, poem titles, a daytime adventure to the nearby Chittenango Falls. But I've unearthed a kind of poetic sequence of them. I thought they would demonstrate a development, a narrative arc. But they didn't! They pick up the same themes from year two to year nine. They are not like a story at all. They are like a loosely written sketchy draft of a numbered section nine-year lyric poem.

Well, what did I expect?

Even in the beginning of my commitment to writing, in the summer of 1959, when I was twelve, I had this experience of believing an image would develop a narrative, then had to realize that no, an image doesn't necessarily produce a story, but it often generates a poem. In that golden pubescent summertime, I went to live with my maternal grandparents who ran a general store and Esso gas station in the tiny hamlet of LaGrange, New York, down the road from the farm where my mother grew up. I had no responsibilities, and entered a kind of shock and displacement, which led to that requisite state of childhood growth: boredom. Only Cazenovia and MacDowell have generated the glory of this boredom. One day, lying on my back in an apple orchard, I was too bored even to daydream. Looking up into the tangle of gray branches above me, a word came to me: "latticework." It was a latticework of branches.

Later I went in to write the word down. I thought maybe I'd make a story of it. But no, it was a single still image. It didn't unfold. It *was*. I wrote a paragraph of description I wish I still had. It was a prose poem.

So, our diary is like that. And here are a few excerpts:

2012.

Monday, July 9th, 2012. PL writes: "Seafood crepes, lamb chops, and a side of yummy spinach cooked with garlic. Right combination in terms of quantity and cost. Molly, Rosé. Phillis, Washington State Merlot. Discussed drafts of M's "The Timothy" and P's "Journey Starting from a Window in a Dream."

July 10th, 2012. MP writes: "We're replicating the MacDowell experience," Phillis says, "Without the difficult people!" We had a minor nervous breakdown about the placement of our table: too much sun, they fluttered around us. What divas we were. But it mattered, as all details do. Then we went to our landing and exchanged poems and talked a bit about Joan. Phillis said, "You spend time at MacDowell looking for friends, but here it's ready made."

July 12th, 2012. PL writes: Breakfast disappointing because we ventured into French toast, too sweet and too seasoned with clove. Pellucid deep, cloudless sky and low humidity. Molly is working on a new poem, "Paid Love." Phillis worked on "Boy with a Book Bag" as well as "Demitasse." Dinner was perfect at table 61. We have the system down. Fabulous shrimp cocktail. Salmon cooked just right with no potatoes. Salad and a side of spinach.

July 13th, 2012. MP writes: Crown of the day our evening walk. Crossed the road in the dark and walked down Carpenter St., passed a bog, drawn by a symphony of bullfrogs. Phillis was nearly screaming (at a whisper, not to disturb) with delight. Met a black cat strolling down Willow Street. Lights on in the nineteenth-century houses, glimpsing fragments of peoples' lives.

July 14th, 2012. MP writes: Bought lettuce on the street at the farmers' market. Met at 6:30 for our last dinner. Arctic Char. Falanghina wine. Phillis's poem "Demitasse." MP poem "Yellow Life." Table 61 on the terrace. Watched the boats come in and the afterglow. We chatted about Anne Michaels' *Fugitive Pieces* which P loved. We were both so moved about our friendship.

2013.

Tuesday, July 9th, 2013. PL writes: Emma's cafe. A quick note because the great unknown is calling us. Yesterday, our first full day with dinner and sunset by the lake, woke today refreshed. Both of us, slept through the night, and are happy and anxious to get to work. We're restored! (From what to what? That's to be learned.)

July 10th, 2013. MP writes: Let's just remember the past couple of days, humid light sprinkles, grayish flash of a goldfinch on Monday morning. Lunch, turkey salad and fresh greens. Talked about Gail, my sister, and about Philip, Phillis's brother. Phillis reminded me that ecstasy means to stand outside yourself.

11 July 2013. MP writes: P & I talked about her childhood. Vigilance prevents a sense of humor.

PL writes: I sat in total contentment, looking out at the bobbing swimmers (including dear Molly.) Dinner table outside not available which was quite distressing. Luckily a table opened up, and we were in heaven. Beet salad with blue cheese. Pinot noir.

Sunday, July 14th, 2013. MP writes: Childhood private games and fantasies: Phillis took Band-aids and reattached leaves to the trees. Her earliest professional desire as a tiny child was to be a plant doctor. Both P and M pretended to be spies. Scrambled eggs and toast. How do we feel our brains change throughout the whole body?

2.

A little interruption and comment: Phillis started writing seriously at age nine, and her poem won honorable mention in the grades four through eight poetry contest for the children of the City of Paterson, judged by Louis Ginsberg. Just think, she was a nine-year-old competing with thirteen-year-olds and still her poem was commended. But her father said, as Phillis quotes from his words' indelible imprint on her memory, "If you'd just have spent another hour on it, you would have won." Ouch.

The poem was about the wind in autumn leaves. My first poem, at age ten, was about the wind of March. So we began at similar ages, with seasons.

In grade seven, my remarkable English teacher, Bernice Baeumler, pushed the Kenmore Public School system to create a literary magazine called *Silver Voices*. In it she published my first poem about "the caprice of the Greek gods." Oh, I loved that new vocabulary word caprice. But not as applied to the capricious demands of parents—though the gods are very much those kinds of parents.

3.

Tuesday, July 16th, 2013. PL writes: So much is beyond words. Dinner last night on the deck outside my room, with food we bought at the farmer's market and smuggled in to make for ourselves was sublime. A salad Molly tossed with her usual genius. Adding artichokes I bought. The lake, the breeze, the mystery of wildflowers. Understanding, humor, soul talk. Bless our good fortune!

2017.
MP writes: Phillis and Molly arrived within half an hour of one another on a brilliant day. Animal watch: 1. Muskrat swimming in the little Willow pond. 2. Land turtle crossing on path after lots of rain. 3. Dragonflies helicoptering at the end of the dock in gray weather. 4. Fireflies on our night walk. 5. A torn up fish on the path, as if a raccoon had left it. 6. Chipmunks scrambled beneath the heaters on the Brewster porch. 7. Huge bullfrog chorus. So loud it sounds like the buzz from a construction site.

Wednesday, July 19th, 2017. PL writes: Choosing poems for *New & Selected*. M working on prose, *Flower Diary*.

Our little diary trails off.

2018.

July 9th, 2018, a year later. MP writes: Emma's Café closed. Now at our new window table at Dave's. Packed, but we found a window seat and had a splendid breakfast, including French toast. It is interesting how we both loved the routine of Emma's, where we were subjected to many rules: no substitutions!!!! Beautiful old booths with red marble tabletops. Yet we found instant advantages at Dave's: Yogurt! Granola! And a certain freedom.

Evenings: The Metal Hour, where the lake looks metallic. The shadows' afterglow of the dropped sun look like sheets of ice. The nights are pleasantly chilly. These routines (the people, the lake, our same rooms, meeting on the landing) all underpin the sense of sanctuary we feel here. Some wonderful individual has created an arch by weaving the branches of live willows over the grass path. Threshold to the writing day.

13 July 2018, PL writes: This time the retreat has been as close to ideal as possible, even better, because it's real. Deep blue skies every morning, low humidity, somewhat cooler weather in general, and a new lushness in the grasses, trees, thistles and the flowers. Maybe more bees too. Read M's chapters on Mary Hiester Reid, and the power of art to change a life's direction. I've managed to salvage a few poems that gave so much trouble I almost abandoned them. Hope to complete several more poems in draft. Untold lines will develop. Emma's on Main is no longer on Main, or anywhere. A small town has room for big things to happen. Or let's say the small things are big in this town.

July 15th, 2018. PL writes: We dined last night at The Seven Stone Steps where invariably we go on a Saturday for dinner. Light drizzle muggy evening. Just enough lamplight for us to read and respond to each other's work. Though exhausted, we walked a bit after driving back in the rain, unlike last year when we got caught in roaring rain.

MP writes: Huge winds blowing to whip up the canvas on the roof of the patio. People running inside, waiters scattering, sheets of rain, the lake silver and roiling. But P and I were tucked in at the table, close to the wall of the house, and we stayed watching the glorious storm roll in: thunder, lightning and then a great calm. Then more thunder, lightning, and the works. We loved it. P has been dealing with her mother in the hospital and written many short poems, all the while commenting daily on my chapters of Mary Hiester Reid.

July 18th our last breakfast. MP writes: Phillis picked the title of my new book: *The Flower Diary of Mary Hiester Reid*. Amazingly, P wrote nine poems, some very small. Every year, we say it's our best year. Nostalgia for the present.

2019.

July 10th, 2019 Wednesday. PL writes: We cited [sic] a great blue heron (truly a great one it was). Molly said, "Let's try this path," one we hadn't yet walked on during this visit to Cazenovia. Lo and behold, through the high grasses, lush willows, in a pool of water, there it was. And it stayed there a long time. And so did we, watching it. At one point it lifted its legs and slowly strode. The joints of its leg were clearly delineated. It bent down with a quick gesture, and dipping its head and long neck, got a fish from the water. We could see the neck change of the heron eating its breakfast for this was morning still. The heron stayed longer, and so did we, until it made a motion to ascend and then flew off. We haven't found this heron again, yet but hope to see it at least once more on this our ninth year here.

MP continues: We sit on the covered patio outside to eat and watch the sunset over the long dock into the lake. And talk about our lives. P's delayed reaction to her father's death, my harrowing spring after Mike's hospitalization and reaction to his drug trial. Of course, I am aware of how privileged we are to be here. And to be able to pay the bill for it.

Scallops, crab cakes, swordfish—and one day, a pizza. Environmental downsides. No one really recycles. A vegetarian would be lost at the Brewster. Huge chartreuse algae blooms on the lake. Is the Brewster like Dove Cottage? Cazenovia our Cotswalds? But there is degradation we almost but can't ignore.

July 16th, 2019. MP writes: Last night Phillis and I must have laughed for three hours at dinner. Worked on my crown of sonnets and tonight P plowed through fourteen of them, laughing at all the funny parts, which got me laughing, and we chuckled and howled through dinner, everything striking us funny, including audio of frog sounds that suddenly went off inside P's bag. She had lots of poems and prose poems, including a frog haiku.

Phillis finishes our diary entry.

PL writes: Last night 15 July 2019, Molly and I had a splendid time at dinner, looking over poems, Molly showed me a sonnet sequence filled with great wit and many streaks of pathos... Quirky and sublime. We laughed. And laughed. In many ways, a refreshing evening. And we had a lovely breeze. Gorgeous... cirrus cloud and absolutely superb lobster roll (mine, minus the roll) the best ever. What more could one ask for? Now it's a bit sad. There are only two full days left in this year's retreat since we leave on Thursday. We have each already written so much and given and received such excellent feedback in our work. The magic of this place. Birdsong galore, darning needles, flitting frog sounds interrupting day and night. The walk on the paths through the high grasses and past the weeping willows brings us to an elsewhere that makes us feel truly home.

Chapter Ten: Trees

Our Cazenovia years were the entrance to our ageing, if ageing can be defined as losing the loved ones who've been mainstays of your life. During our Caz retreats, I thought about environmental damage and Charlotte Mew's line "Hurt not the trees" from her magnificent poem, "The Trees Are Down," at the same time as I was suffering a massive case of what psychologist Pauline Boss would call "ambiguous loss." Ambiguous loss is the state of grief a person experiences when a loved one "goes missing." It's what spouses of soldiers missing in action feel, the lack of closure of the person's death, the possibility that the beloved could actually turn up again. It's what a person experiences when a loved one begins to disappear into Alzheimer's disease, or, in my case, when Joan Stein's sharp insight and verbal acuity disappeared after her stroke. Ambiguous loss was also what I was beginning to experience with my husband. As his illness wore on, and as I took up many of the tasks that he performed in our marriage, I was losing the person he was. At some point (not one I can exactly point out, though), as with Joan, the full person of Mike vanished and died before he did.

Great trees of my life were being felled. So, when Mew writes,

> They are cutting down the great planetrees at the end
>   of the gardens.
> For days there has been the grate of the saw, the
> swish of the branches as they fall,
> The crash of trunks, the rustle of trodden leaves,

I am pierced again with the losses of Joan and Mike, both of whom have now passed away. Trees have human shapes, trunks for bodies and arms that reach to the sky. Inevitably we identify them as human. Toward the end of the poem Mew writes,

> It is not for a moment the Spring is unmade today;
> These were great trees, it was in them from root to stem:

The actual felling of the trees erases ambiguity from the loss. Now their absence is comfortingly clear, and a whole season on earth, Spring, is "unmade." I have to mention the rat in this poem. Without the rat, the poem wouldn't have nearly its resonance. The "old dead rat," too, had a singular life. The rat makes the poem about a world of losses, both magnificent and in mud.

> I remember thinking: alive or dead, a rat was a god-
>   forsaken thing,
> But at least, in May, that even a rat should be alive.

Here's the whole poem, with its classist, snobby reference to the tree cutters, who, yes, are agents of evil, but also ordinary working-class guys, "common," with their "Whoops" and "Whoas." Those men, like my father, just had a job to do.

THE TREES ARE DOWN
by Charlotte Mew (1869-1928)

—and he cried with a loud voice:
Hurt not the earth, neither the sea, nor the trees—
(Revelation)

They are cutting down the great planetrees at the end
of the gardens.
For days there has been the grate of the saw, the
    swish of the branches as they fall,
The crash of trunks, the rustle of trodden leaves,
With the 'Whoops' and the 'Whoas,' the loud common
talk, the loud common laughs of the men, above it all.

I remember one evening of a long past Spring
Turning in at a gate, getting out of a cart, and find-
    ing a large dead rat in the mud of the drive.
I remember thinking: alive or dead, a rat was a god-
    forsaken thing,
But at least, in May, that even a rat should be alive.

The week's work here is as good as done. There is just
    one bough
      On the roped bole, in the fine grey rain,
          Green and high
          And lonely against the sky.
              (Down now!—)
          And but for that,
          If an old dead rat
Did once, for a moment, unmake the Spring, I might
    never have thought of him again.

It is not for a moment the Spring is unmade today;
These were great trees, it was in them from root to stem:
When the men with the 'Whoops' and the 'Whoas' have
    carted the whole of the whispering loveliness away
Half the Spring, for me, will have gone with them.

It is going now, and my heart has been struck with the
    hearts of the planes;
Half my life it has beat with these, in the sun, in the rains,
In the March wind, the May breeze,
In the great gales that came over to them across the
    roofs from the great seas.
There was only a quiet rain when they were dying;
They must have heard the sparrows flying,
And the small creeping creatures in the earth where
    they were lying—
But I, all day, I heard an angel crying:
'Hurt not the trees.'[16]

Mew's poem provoked me to consider two other tree poems, "To the Forest" by Phillis, who, incidentally, wanted to be a tree doctor when she was a little girl, and "The Nurse Tree," a poem of my own. If any two poems would distinguish the difference between Levin and Peacock, it might be these.

    "To the Forest" is mythic and fairy-tale like—and mysterious. It begins with a cataclysm: "A tree fell on me." The speaker also turns out to be a tree and "thrashes" with the fallen tree, introducing a play on "rose" that has a dream-like connection to the needles—oh, they must be pines!—dotting the trees' arms. As with dreams, I don't fully understand the poem. It seems psychologically urgent, and it seems true to the altered sense of time and space in dreams. A tree falls. There are other trees. And they talk about a "She" who is many. And her skin is burnt. A rose rises up, and it lives. A woodsman appears, understands that a terrifying splitting has occurred, and declares that the tree must be "cut" in punishment for what it has done. The poem seems to me like a glass sculpture that I keep turning and turning in my hand seeing angle after angle. It is impenetrable, but also invites re-reading. As in Charlotte Mew's poem, where the tree subject is made all the richer by the rat, here the tree subject is made all the richer by the rose that is "broken but full" and "would not die." The daring wordplay and line breaks of "It/ be-/ fell:// a bell" interrupt the poem just the way "And but for that/ if an old dead rat" interrupt "The Trees Are Down." Shortening the lines, cinching them in almost as a belt cinches a waistline, is thrilling and adds a wide dimension to each poem, for each poem spills out of its stanza form. And both poems are so musical! They change rhythms as swiftly as water.[17]

To the Forest
by Phillis Levin

A tree fell on me. There is no other way
to say this. I do not want to explain.
It fell. And I too was a tree, and together

we were thrashing, and it seemed
the sap rose and the rose's thorn—

no, the needles
brushed
against me.

I do not want to say,

I cannot say
this
any other way.

It should be said
only to make it go away.

A tree fell
and rose, and together
we swept the sky.

And one of the other trees said:
I recall someone walking among us,
how she was taken, how it seemed she was
one of us, and then how it seemed
all of us had been like her,

but no, it cannot be,
we are stalwart.

She wanted something to happen
but nothing like that,
she wanted everything but no,
not that,

she didn't want anything at all.

She is many,
as is every
tree
a story of one
and many.

Without a sound it crashed,
burning my skin,
my mouth.

And afterward a rose appeared,
broken but full, and I
carried it home and woke to see it there
and thought it would die but it would not die,

it wanted to be there remembering itself,
mocking the daylight with its blush.

It
be-
fell:

a bell
rang
without sounding,
its tongue
melting
my tongue.

The woodsman said,
the tree must be cut
that did this,

whatever has done this to you
will be split
in two.

But my own tree poem, "The Nurse Tree," is both more casual and more regular. I had read in a Tuesday *New York Times* science section—my favorite section of the entire print *Times* all week, and much perused by Phillis, too—about the concept of "nurse trees," fallen trees that nurture other growth in the forest. I loved the idea so much that I held it in my mind. Just holding an idea results in an image that can drive a poem. I thought of Joan Stein as a nurse tree. She had fallen, but I had grown from her. This was such a positive thought after the tragedy of the stroke that took away her language but didn't take away her ability to paint and draw. In her falling, she showed me how, eventually, to fall. For we all fall. That is the poignancy of the trees in Mew's poem, and that is the fight in Levin's poem. Levin thrashes with death. Mew mourns it. I don't always but, in "The Nurse Tree" I search for the positive in deathly transformation.

THE NURSE TREE
by Molly Peacock

Why waste away in a box
when you could be a nurse tree?
That's what they call dead logs:
mushroomeries of the woods.

Your living room's a wood
of couches, books, and chairs.
You're dead not at all, but
could you be preparing

for things to grow inside
the chest of the log
you plan to become:
cherished compost heap

where heat turns the brown
mess of feelings, sorry,
that's *peelings*, into comp-o-
sition? For we who love

our hands in dirt, a leaf skirt
*de*composing seems an ideal
station between this life and
next: I visit your room

as on a forest walk. Passing
a fallen log—is that you?—
I see a scarlet fungus cap
pop up from friable bark.

"Why waste away in a box?" begins with a coffin, but immediately gives an alternative. Joan is the "you" in the poem. There I am in her living room, while she is turning into a nurse tree, and the living room becomes a forest. There's a blithe, upbeat tone to the poem, and lots of fun wordplay from my invented "mushroomeries" to "feelings/ peelings" to "de-composing." The poem is about transforming. It's on the way to death, but it's also on the way to the surprise of insight and new knowledge. There's a regularity in the quatrains, unlike the Mew or Levin poems. Yet "The Nurse Tree" is related to them. Those poems were not particularly in my mind as I wrote, but they lingered in the distant clouds.

Also, my vocabulary is earthy; horticulture is a deep interest of mine, and part of my attachment to it is luscious vocabulary like "friable." A private aside: the "scarlet fungus cap" reminds me of the red robes in the medieval paintings Joan loved at the Frick Museum.

Chapter Eleven:
Credo

When I asked Phillis if she has a signature poem, something that would be a credo, she landed on a new poem, "An Anthology of Rain." Perfect! The drops of rain on the window, corresponding to the drops of rain in the first poem of her first book, testify to Levin's consistency of vision, her understanding of the sources of her imagination and her body of work. She enters into an almost Socratic dialog with her reader as she constructs that paradoxical concept, an anthology of rain. Much of poetry is encountered in anthologies. But you can't leave an anthology out in the rain, can you? What if the anthology (what if poetry itself) is rain? Levin knows that this idea is outwardly absurd and inwardly a matter of common sense, where you are "free to say/ Whatever crosses your mind." The experience of the mind freeing itself is the quintessential quality of a Levin poem, especially this one:

AN ANTHOLOGY OF RAIN
by Phillis Levin

For this you may see no need,
You may think my aim
Dead set on something

Devoid of conceivable value:
An Anthology of Rain,
A collection of voices

Telling someone somewhere
What it means to follow a drop
Traveling to its final place of rest.

But do consider this request
If you have pressed your nose
Of any shape against a window,

Odor of metal faint, persistent,
While a storm cast its cloak
Over the shoulder of every cloud

In sight. You are free to say
Whatever crosses your mind
When you look at the face of time

In the passing of one drop
Gathering speed, one drop
Chasing another, racing it to

A fork in the path, lingering
Before making a detour to join
Another, fattening on the way

Until entering a rivulet
Running to the sill.
So please accept this invitation:

You are welcome to submit,
There is no limit to its limit,
The instructions are a breeze

As long as you include
Nothing about yourself,
Even your name. Your address

Remains unnecessary, for the rain
Will find you—if you receive it
It receives you (whether or not

You contribute, a volume
Is sent). And when you lift
The collection you may hear,

By opening anywhere, a drop
And its story reappear
As air turns to water, water to air.

From the onset Levin knows that you, the audience, might think an anthology of rain has no "conceivable value." But what of its *in*-conceivable value? What if you have to go beyond conceiving to get to the value? What if you have to free your mind to get there? "But do consider this request," she says to us, her readers, as she posits an argument for this mental freedom. Yet her argument dissolves into a description of a raindrop's geometry, a "Telling" to "someone somewhere/ What it means to follow a drop/ Traveling to its final place of rest." As Levin depicts "one drop/ Gathering speed, one drop/ Chasing another," she lets you "look at the face of time" until you become "free to say/ Whatever crosses your mind."

By the way, you'll notice that Levin capitalizes every line. (Peacock, on the other hand, almost never does.) Yet neither of us feels we have to be consistent; we let the poem determine that. Levin carves the line; she speaks every line to herself, evolving the poem musically. And a final note, Levin uses tercets in this poem, that most ethereal of stanzas.

When I asked myself the Credo question, I thought of a poem that I placed last, and culminatively, in *Cornucopia: New and Selected Poems*. So, it is not a brand-new poem, but one I have read over and over again to audiences, and one that anchored *The Shimmering Verge*. Like "An Anthology of Rain," "Why I Am Not a Buddhist" is an argument, a kind of soft plea for the positive benefits of desire, that desire is not craving, but spiritual, that having is prerequisite to giving. That's why "building a kingdom in a soul/ requires desire." This sonnet-like poem of eighteen lines (a quatrain is added to complete the thought) rapidly accumulates images of a "beltless bathrobe," "tongues of cash," a "mauve suit," a "loved pen," and a nut cake, affording all the senses satisfaction. Then the poet ranks them in priority, but insists on the meaning of each, nonetheless.

WHY I AM NOT A BUDDHIST
by Molly Peacock

I love desire, the state of want and thought
of how to get; building a kingdom in a soul
requires desire. I love the things I've sought—
you in your beltless bathrobe, tongues of cash that loll
from my billfold—and love what I want: clothes,
houses, redemption. Can a new mauve suit

equal God? Oh no, desire is ranked. To lose
a loved pen is not like losing faith. Acute
desire for nut gateau is driven out by death,
but the cake on its plate has meaning,
even when love is endangered and nothing matters.
For my mother, health; for my sister, bereft,
wholeness. But why is desire suffering?
Because want leaves a world in tatters?
How else but in tatters should a world be?
A columned porch set high above a lake.
Here, take my money. A loved face in agony
the spirit gone. Here, use my rags of love.

Using the proportion of the sonnet, Peacock turns these ideas when she suddenly introduces the anguish of her mother and sister, then asks a key question, "But why is desire suffering?" Now the reader is deep into an argument; but, like Levin's "Anthology of Rain," the argument is a discourse of the ephemeral. Peacock gives the answer by posing two questions that don't need answers. "Because want leaves a world in tatters?" she asks. Then she responds in league with the reader, saying confidentially, "How else but in tatters should a world be?"

Suddenly a new image comes in, conjuring up Cazenovia (though the poem was written before the Cazenovia sojourns): "A columned porch set high above a lake." The poet is willing to spend her money for that respite. This in turn is followed by the ultimate caregiving demand: "A loved face in agony/ the spirit gone." At last, the poet answers with a little echo of W. B. Yeats' "foul rag and bone shop of the heart." "Here, use my rags of love." Her answer is to give all you've got, even the rag-ends.

Typically, Peacock uses the line as a rhythmic underpinning; she does not want the reader to be conscious of the line in the onrush of the collection of sensory experiences accumulating. More importantly, she enjambs lines because she does not want a reader to be too conscious of her poem's rhyme scheme. She wants a reader to feel the way through.

The contrasting nature of these poems (in one, the rain's rivulets on glass, and in the other, a sensualist's choices of clothes and houses) belies their similar tactic. Each poem argues for a mental or emotional state. One sets up a situation for freeing the mind. The other proposes freeing desire so that the ultimate price of love (in Peacock's mind, this is caregiving) may be paid. The poems offer a dialog, an exchange. When Levin drolly issues "this invitation" as if to a poetry anthology, "You are welcome to submit,/ There is no limit to its limit," she plays with freedom. On the other hand, Peacock begins with the freedom to want things, though she ends in limitations—even as those limitations free an individual to experience the depth of love.

Chapter Twelve:
Fax & Future

1.

In the same way that doctors' offices still use that outmoded lump of a charcoal gray metal machine, the Fax, so do Phillis and I. It's like being committed to a typewriter, or a flip phone, or a vintage car. When the gravelly purr of my fax machine goes on, I know it can only be Phillis. Some years ago, when my husband was still alive, our Fax wasn't working properly. Because the cords ran underneath an enormous bookcase that would have had to be dismantled and moved, and because Phillis was the only faxer (with weeks, even months, between faxing sessions, which always had the slight quality of an emergency since that antiquated sound was so infrequent), it went unrepaired. Probably Mike was hoping against hope that these difficulties would train Phillis to use a new technology, but he underestimated the stubbornness of a true Taurus like PL. At last, with days of disruption, we replaced it.

Faxing weds Phillis and me to paper, and our eyes don't have to slide off screens. Phillis doesn't have to reinjure her shoulder again and again. I don't have to invite an ocular migraine from screen overuse. And there is the luxury of the pen in the hand, the typeface, and the friend's setup on the page, with our handwriting and Phillis's elaborate lettering system of alternatives to line breaks and vocabulary that are so manifold they are migraine-worthy in themselves. But they prompt a phone conversation, and then we sit down, on a subsequent morning where we have breakfast on the phone as if we had stayed overnight at one or the other's house— and we talk in the same way that we would talk at a table.

It's not the absolute same, though. It's a substitute for not seeing each other, almost like the substitute sweater for the favorite I lost. The replacement is good enough, but not as sweet. Yet PL and I yammer on, and because we have a short time to focus, given the other demands of our days, we solve problems and come away thanking one another.

2.

Because neither Phillis nor I have easily rolled from success to success, gratitude has come to play a role. Phillis, who had published poems in *The New Yorker* and other major journals, had great trouble getting her second manuscript accepted in the brief time frame of tenure pressure in her university department. She was rescued by Copper Beech Press. After my initial success with *The New Yorker*, two consecutive editors turned me down for twenty years, but with W. W. Norton and Company I thrived. Success really is 95% persistence. I do not know what made us keep going exactly, but I do know enthusiasm for each other's work helped. I can confidently say, "This is one of the best things you've ever written," because I've actually read most of everything Phillis has ever written after the age of twenty-two. In some ways, that might be our lasting strength. Almost every word, wrested from a preverbal or a nonverbal state has come from us to each other's eyes. With each poem we see from one another, we can wonder at its development, because it is a surprise, even as it is predictable in form or shape. The way dreams startle you, yet remain recognizable as dreams, so our poems are unpredictable, yet they retain our characteristics. It's a Phillis poem, or a Molly poem. We're not bored by them.

Phillis's habits could—and can—enrage me as only a sister figure can. Sometimes I think *Could you just act like a normal person?* Someone who would text a short text, not a five-hundred-word whale-text? Someone who could sense what's proportional in social interaction the way she can sense what's proportional in a poem? Someone who didn't call and dump all the detritus of her life on me for twenty full minutes before she asks me how I am? But my resentment fades in the quality of her attention. Besides, why on earth would I expect such an unusual person as Phillis to be so-called normal? In the realm of poetry, we are balanced and graceful. Like two Olympic skaters meeting again and again on the ice with two distinct styles, we have a huge respect for the hours of practice and the genius of skill that has made each of us who we are. This is a special kind of aesthetic love. We know instinctively that we must take care of it the way we take care of our poetry. It is both fragile and as bendable as a Cazenovia willow.

And there is something that Phillis gives me that I need. In the nearly thirty years that my writing life filled out with a memoir and then with a new skill set as a biographer, and with a demanding and fulfilling marriage to a prominent scholar, and with a public literary life sometimes in three countries, Phillis anchored me to poetry. There were times when I did not think I would write poetry except for my appointments with her. She returns me to an essential part of my existence.

Carrying on my fish metaphor, here's a poem I wrote about this process as it pertains to PL and MP. In it, Phillis cooks a fish, and we both eat it. Now I realize it's another version of "died with the fishes."

OLD FRIENDS
by Molly Peacock

One waiting, one attending. Patience.
Now a gift will be delivered. Her food
from her hands. Her turn tonight. All the good
little dishes assembled and friendship hence
ever so slightly adjusted in level.
No one grows evenly. One surges. One lags.
But here comes a resting point. All
focus on a platter: two sole almost wag
their tails, so happy are they to be served.
Lovely. Think so? Thank you. Our pleasure
crosses and re-crosses, making cursive
loops as if written on paper, a measure
of lines made by our lives as they swerve by
making letters. My meal. Her meal. A missive.

Though we rarely cook together, we talk about cooking and sometimes talk on the phone while we *are* cooking. Ukrainian borscht is one of the things each of us has made, with great effort. We're always on the hunt to have a soup at home that somewhat resembles the rich vegetable-y borscht we would get at the Ukrainian National Home and, later, at Veselka on Second Avenue. After a funeral for our friend the poet Liam Rector at St. Marks Church on a sweltering September day, we repaired to Veselka and ate steamy borscht to console ourselves. Phillis cooked borscht on her tiny stove in the West Village decades ago, and for about ten Decembers before my husband died, he and I made Ukrainian borscht and ate it during the holidays. (Mike was an excellent chopper, and our recipe took at least two people's labor.) Whenever Phillis and I see a beet salad on a menu, we know that's one of the things we're going to get. The red beets go straight to our blood-streams, and Phillis has a juicy poem about them.

BEETS
by Phillis Levin

Take them in your hands and peel them
Until shades of red darken your skin,
Get under your nails, as at last you succumb
To understanding that making borscht

Leads to nothing less than accepting the stain
Of the earth, its signs in freckles spotting
Your face, marking the cookbook's margin.
Rubies will soon appear: wet jewels

That live underground until someone digging
Past ruddy leaves lifts them into the sun
Before they are sent to where you buy them,
Bound and sleeping in dust.

Grating is an exercise in boredom,
So you listen to Handel or look out a window
Until you scrape a knuckle and finally see
To finish a task is to stay with it completely,

Knowing it will end if you take your time.
After this, meat seems superfluous,
Almost revolting, but the bone must go in
And cook, until it falls into shreds.

It's these five lines that have the pith of advice:

> Grating is an exercise in boredom,
> So you listen to Handel or look out a window
> Until you scrape a knuckle and finally see
> To finish a task is to stay with it completely,
>
> Knowing it will end if you take your time.

Grating your knuckles on something, well, sometimes I think choosing the life of the poet is grating your knuckles on the whole North American culture. And writing a poem means that "To finish a task is to stay with it completely,/ Knowing it will end if you take your time." One loses track of time when writing a poem; but more importantly, writing a poem means one has taken time, of all the things in the world that one must do, and inversely, the poem gives time back.

3.

Of course, we don't always have time for one another, or even have the capacity to identify with what one another is experiencing. Phillis has never taken care of an extremely ill, adored husband, or had to help him die. I could not rely on her personally during my husband's final illness and turned to my friends who are widows or whose husbands were ill. But I knew Phillis would get the poems I wrote about my extreme loss. And I needed that more than anything. "Do I have to perform for your friendship?" Phillis, wounded when I once described our friendship as a poetry friendship, asked me. *Of course not!* I reassured her. Yet our friendship is so unusual that there really is an aspect of performing, at least performing as a reader for one another. Because the mirroring that we do for one another is the mirroring of written language, not the mirroring of experience.

Now that my husband has passed away, I have deliberately and affectionately anchored my life in a condominium in Toronto to face what I thought would be the curiosities of my ageing. But the best curiosity is: I feel so alive! I never expected this renewed vigor at seventy-five. I play badminton against a fifty-year-old opponent—and sometimes win. In low-Covid intervals I travel, give readings, and find myself continually cooking for friends. In the mornings I draft poems and make cartoons—when I'm not working on the Michael Groden Archives. My balcony garden flourishes, and a bit of romance has entered my life. But where is Phillis?

Her life, too, is expanding. She and her husband have a new house and garden in Connecticut; she has new poems, and perhaps a *New and Selected* after she retires from teaching. I wonder what will happen to us after these changes, but I don't wonder how our friendship will survive. We will figure it out.

"I'll figure it out," Phillis says after I have brought up several issues in a poem she is working on.

"You'll figure it out," I say when I feel I have touched a tender limit of some narrative that is unclear to me, but whose fog seems necessary in a way I don't understand in Phillis's poem.

The creative solution will emerge. And I won't know where it will emerge from. Just that it will be a surprise to me.

Is that what the steadiness and rigor of all rituals lead to? The reward of surprise?

Friendship
by Molly Peacock

On not knowing what you need

I cannot choose a friend intentionally.
I've tried, when I've needed a friend in a crowd,
to pick the person, but my choice and me
work only in the flattery stage, the wow
of being wanted. It shocks me when it frays
because I'm convinced I know what I need.
But at my side some person in the bluish haze
of the not-quite-ignored and I begin to read
one another almost as a scent is read
before the rain—minerals in the soil—
and I'm led as the other is led
to some stray but mutual remark as it uncoils
from an almost infinite spool, though it's just a thread
then, like a little orange thread off a pair of jeans,
oh, of course nothing's what it seems—why don't
I see that? After years, the close friend who emerged
from a fog at my side recalls a want
so hidden from me, it seemed itself a fog.

"Friendship" is a new poem, and of course Phillis saw it
evolving. We agreed that it was a good idea *not* to use that
delicious but far too fancy word "petrichor" in the tenth line.
Instead, I stuck with an ordinary phrase, "minerals in the
soil." After all, what I wanted was a scent, not a concept.

5.

Although my mother Pauline Ruth Wright Peacock and Phillis's mother Charlotte Shirley Engel Levin had very little in common, the Rosenberg spy case and the McCarthy hearings had a powerful influence on both—resulting in their warnings to us as little girls growing up in the McCarthy Era.

"Don't ever sign anything!" my mother said to me—I must have been five at the time—and repeated this admonition in fear when I was seven, ten, fifteen, twenty, thirty-five, forty, till she said, when I was forty-five years old, and she was dying, "You haven't signed anything, have you? Don't sign. You could lose everything." Of Ethel Rosenberg, whom my mother admired, she said, "She's tough." The picture of her walking to her death was indelible. Charlotte Levin also reinforced the Polly rule to Phillis: don't sign. You'll ruin your life.

With every petition I've signed in all my years, with every march for human rights I've joined, my mother's admonition rings in my ears, as well as her admiration for people who *did* stand up. "She's tough." Well, I don't know how tough I am. Or how tough Phillis turned out to be. But there is a certain fierce determination to us, even though signing contracts and legal documents sends an irrational frisson through me.

I believe a person has to have a very permeable skin as a poet. You must be able to feel the world, even as you have to protect your gift from that very world. Inevitably you will be hurt. The amount of rejection you endure is enormous and a daily fact. Marianne Moore is reputed to have said that she didn't feel it was all over for publishing a poem until she had sent it out forty times. I'm sure my mother would have applied the "She's tough" label to Marianne Moore. Between "don't sign" and "she's tough" is the course of a life, well, two lives, since luck let me make a friend of Phillis Levin.

In an undated notebook of ours, the first page of which bears the title *Two Solitudes*, there are a handful of notes. I must have been jotting down a conversation we were having about revision. "REVISION IS HOPE," Phillis said, "you see the possibility of resurrection." So, *Rejection can also mean resurrection,* I scribbled. Then Phillis said about revising a poem, "It doesn't have to be on fire; the poem can take fire later." Tucked in this notebook is a clipping from *The New Yorker*, page 75, February 25th, 2013. Rilke, in a letter made the same point: "I hold this to be the highest task for a bond between two people: that each protects the solitude of the other."

I feel, as our mothers thought they were protecting us with "don't sign," that we protect each other—and our solitudes—with the encouragement to sign and to revise the sign, again and again.

6.

When I titled the translation of the riddle "Ship's Figurehead," I didn't quite believe it *was* the actual solution. *That's* what the riddler was talking about? *That's* the gray queen? Yet I could envision on the prow of the ship, so mysterious, the carved figure that had the loneliness of a man alone (for me, my mother's expression, "she's tough" somehow equates to "a man, solo") in the middle of an ocean, no land in sight, who both flew with the birds and simultaneously swam. (That simultaneity seems to me how metaphor functions, holding at once two images, ideas, and feelings, as if you both stayed on one side of a mirror *and* also walked through that mirror to stare back from the other side.) To dive under and to die, then to step out on earth (a shore has been reached!) alive, despite everything and because of everything, "all in a single soul." That is the friend's ship, the single soul that Phillis and

I share when we meet at a table with papers in our hands.

What happens now that the pandemic's changes and death's changes have ended our years in Cazenovia? Worse, has my articulating our process ruined it? But metaphor doesn't ruin a thought, because metaphor only suggests, it doesn't over-define. Riddles are, in themselves, questions that live inside a beauty that exists even when you can't answer them. That riddle, one of the earliest poems in English that we have, survives without its answer. It's really nice to have the suggestion of "Ship's Figurehead," but even so, it's an ambiguous response. Who can be sure it's correct? Conscientious Anglo-Saxon scholars came up with the answer, but still, they could have been wrong. For Phillis and for myself, to be alive is to inhabit contradictions. You're never going to get a bottom-line definition from either of us. We meet in the land of ambiguity, as P says in her last Cazenovia diary entry, the "elsewhere that is home."

We don't need our retreat in the same way that we did when we were suffering so many losses. But I miss it. After all, when I think of my two favorite words, "summer evening,"[18] I don't think of spending those evenings alone.

7.

As I write this, Phillis and I have seen each other once, at Altesi restaurant in New York, after almost two pandemic years. It was the week our mentor, Richard Howard, died at ninety-two. I am seventy-five, and Phillis, sixty-eight. We settled in the orange leather chairs and ordered a feast: Vitello tonnato, salmon with fennel and dill, sautéed artichokes with zucchini and shrimp. Two glasses of Falanghina.

We mused about our fathers. They both had workshops. We both watched them build things. Precision was involved. A mechanical creature, like an electric saw, came to life.

We thought about how precision is so important to poetry. Phillis was wearing a gray and pale blue print top I have seen her wear for years with her signature black skirt. I was wearing my signature black pencil pants with a blue jacket and a periwinkle and yellow scarf. We returned to our theme of mirrors. Rhyme really is a mirror where you see sound as well as hear it, I mused as Phillis remembered putting two mirrors together as a child. "It's where interiority and exteriority meet," she said.

Then we started on the artichokes.

Afterword

"There is no Frigate like a Book"
—Emily Dickinson, #1263

"A subject cannot constitute itself without a constituent object."
—György Lukács

DO YOU READ ME?

My favorite childhood toy was a battery-operated globe that rotated on its axis: a metal mechanism revolved around it, blowing a steady stream of air on which a ping pong ball was suspended—the moon, orbiting the earth. That contraption informs the closing stanza of my poem "Something About Windows," reprinted in the first chapter of this book. But it was an image, a photograph of a park in Paris with a grove of chestnut trees and a vanishing point suggesting the infinite, that provoked the poem into being, its opening lines arriving from a prelinguistic elsewhere that often is poetry's source. My desire to touch the world, explore the globe, began long ago; so did my desire for friendship, for kinship with another soul. What great fortune to have a poet-friend so alive to nuance, so open to sharing and renewal.

A friend sails in on a poem. The horizon is beloved, familiar; in whatever weather, what appears emerges first in the distance, growing clearer and clearer as the form moves into sight. And we know this vessel will bring the thrill of surprise, that the cargo it carries will be rich and strange, that it will change before our eyes, and that the more our attention holds it, the more it will unfold.

*

When I read an earlier draft of *A Friend Sails in on a Poem,* I realized that in addition to portraying our literary friendship, Molly was making a self-portrait—and a portrait of me, as well, as a person in time, apart from my work on the page, connecting the dots as best she could, deploying knowledge and impressions she gleaned over the decades we have known each other. As our lives transformed, as we became more and more ourselves, we always cherished an absolute belief in each other's talent, whatever else was brewing or looming personally, professionally. Sometimes I didn't recognize the person she was depicting, or the milieu in which she thought I had been raised. Molly grasped the atmosphere, but sometimes the circumstances were different from what she imagined. Why does it matter for the record to be accurate? I can write my own memoir, after all. Molly was filling in the blanks because she didn't have certain vital information, things undisclosed in conversation though not withheld. She knew my poems well, had read almost everything I composed after turning twenty-two; but much in my life remained unspoken or hidden, despite the troves of recollection we shared.

In a few instances, the discrepancy between imagination and actuality was a gift. Molly's memory of our weekly poetry workshop at Johns Hopkins included a strand of pearls she bestowed on me retroactively, for they came into my possession several decades later. And a ring that for years was the only piece of jewelry I wore encircled a finger of my hand before I purchased it: this lovely little mosaic, depicting the dove of the Holy Spirit, which I found in a shop in Florence a few years after Molly and I first met, became emblematic—as if Molly's misremembering *when* that ring became mine revealed her wish for me to have something I wanted (and her intuition that I'd have trouble allowing myself to possess what I desired, especially anything material, though she cautioned I was too easily smitten by beauty). For much of her life, Molly has painted as well as written poetry, finding the craft of the visual artist a refreshing source of delight; like a painter, she made a portrait incorporating her multi-layered sense of the person I was, perceived over time, in different lights. The constant that runs through the time we know each other is our trust that each will give the other's work a depth of attention transcending appreciation, inhabit the other's playing field for a while, be nonjudgmental in response yet unafraid to offer a finely calibrated judgment. Molly's process of writing this book, and my process of reading it, led us to acknowledge the wealth of what remains unknown: in discovering other differences and distances, we built a new bridge between us.

*

Initial impression of Molly: an adult who was divorced and owned a car, who had already held a full-time job and attended an artist residency—all these accomplishments before the age of thirty. A careful, caring person who gathered her thoughts before she spoke, whose remarks were cogent and crisp, candid, on target. A person with clear contours, who defended her boundaries. For me, not having an older or younger sister meant there was no sister dynamic in my psyche to repeat or resist (I have one sibling, a younger brother, so being protective and being first born were familiar). Once I learned about Molly's troubled sister and the turmoil that relationship created, an ongoing burden compounded by the fear and fact of her father's erratic often violent behavior, I became hyperaware of how the weight of responsibility threatened to rupture Molly's life. It takes enormous energy and skill to ward off danger, even more energy and skill to preserve one's integrity, stay whole, and be vitally creative, when struggling to survive. Paradoxically, as Molly got older, she seemed younger, she relaxed into being herself, softened in relation to others. One by one, burdens lifted, levity replaced severity. But not all attachments are burdens, and without any responsibility to another human being most of us feel unmoored. Friendship anchors us and gives us leeway to sail.

Who was I when Molly first got to know me? I still felt porous, could be anyone, yet knew who I was at the core, a core formed in early childhood—through the act of looking, observing, absorbing what I heard and saw, studying faces, flowers, leaves—a core affirmed, by the age of nine, in the act of writing, my soul incarnate on a page. Passages of prose entered my diary at great speed; poems arose from my body, beginning as breath, rhythm seeking a sonic shape. At the same time, my perceptions were being undermined: even as a small child my inner life, my privacy and evident interiority, provoked in both parents, especially my mother, a burgeoning fear that increased their attempts to know what went on in my mind. Disclosing a thought usually caused trouble; thus, I learned to keep to myself, be inaccessible. My poems could be direct or circuitous in their syntax, but subjective utterance was disguised or embodied in analogy and metaphor. Any expression of individuality, of an independent will, was taken as a sign of rebellion. "Every true poet is a monster," begins "Folk Song" by Tomaž Šalamun. No wonder that line rang so true: I felt dangerous; though people outside my family described me as kind and good by nature, I felt like a monster, was called one, and believed that this was my genuine nature (and eventually would be revealed). By sixth grade I began to speak my mind, practice reasoned arguments that hit a wall of unreason; I never ran away from home—but considered it. A few months after graduating from Sarah Lawrence College, the intellectual home that set me free, I arrived in Baltimore weeks before classes began and euphorically worked on poems many hours each day into the night. My desk consisted of a door and two filing cabinets my father brought along in the car and assembled in my room, though he and my mother worried I was starting to waste my life. How lucky I was to land in class with Molly, Rachel Hadas, Tom Sleigh, and Lisa Zeidner, to know with certitude that in each other's company we could flourish, be inspired, belong.

I didn't feel young, and adults with whom I spoke considered me wise beyond my years. But I felt infinite potential: the future imagined wasn't personal, no fantasy of marriage and family; though I had experienced several intense romantic attachments, those relations existed in a parallel realm, apart from my artistic ambitions and, until my mid-twenties, my interest in becoming a psychologist or scientist. Rarely allowed to play with other children, I occupied myself with reading voraciously and imagining a future in which I would be a great poet and a hero who brought peace to the world. My being female did not affect my parents' assumptions that I would succeed professionally; but when they realized how serious I was about being a writer, they grew alarmed, fearing I would never have financial stability; my unwavering focus on poetry concerned them even more. Though they took pride in my literary accomplishments, only after I was a tenured professor did they relax a bit, and only after I married did they show acceptance. To this day, I have an aversion to being defined by a preconceived category, be it gender, religion, or aesthetic style: I do not—and do not want to—fit in a box. But in kindergarten, I would stand in line in the playground, praying to be like the other children, wondering why I didn't fit in, why they thought me different.

*

The struggle to be free: from what, exactly? And for what, to what end? Perhaps, to no end in sight. It has been different for each of us, in different moments of our lives. For the poem to be its fullest expression of itself. We each have been witness to this struggle in the other—as individuals and as poets. Often, the work could achieve what the person could not. When I look back on the many poems I composed before the age of eighteen, I marvel at how they knew what would take a few more decades to learn. Likewise, it's possible that Molly intuited aspects of my future life before I began to live those moments. Being born seven years apart was significant, but eventually that difference faded. I had been wise for as long as I remained detached from my emotions; as time progressed it seemed I knew less and less until something shifted, transformed: Molly was there to welcome me again, to recognize and accept.

*

"Life's cache is flesh, flesh, and flesh." Those words on the page from her sonnet "The Lull," and the memory of Molly performing them with relish—her inflection conveying the tragic and joyous consequence of our earthly state—continue to resound. No escaping the limit of the body; no escaping how a poem stops time by keeping time. Vulnerability, awe, and power define our approach to the making of authentic art, intermingle in our day to day lives. Only lately have I felt mortal; the recent death of both my parents, who looked and seemed much younger than their years until time's toll overtook them quite suddenly, and the loss of several close friends who also seemed immortal, philosopher and linguist Elfie Raymond, poet Tomaž Šalamun and then Tomaž's wife, the painter Metka Krašovec, shook the ground of being, altered my perspective if not my character and soul, in a way it does for most people much earlier. Not as dramatically, yet substantially, the end of our yearly ritual of going to Cazenovia unsettled me, was difficult to face, though I accepted the verdict as soon as Molly announced it. Her husband Mike was too ill. Another pandemic summer arrived; the border between Canada and the United States was closed. And when it reopened, we still would not return.

Preparing for our time at The Brewster Inn meant gathering rough drafts and almost-finished poems (and for Molly, chapters of a new biography, as well), knowing that something new, not yet imagined, would arise. Walking with Molly to town for an early breakfast and meeting her for a summer-sunset dinner overlooking the lake, after working long hours in our separate, fruitful solitudes: those two set events bracketed our day. And we anticipated the creative work that would commence in our after-dinner conversation in response to new drafts we brought to the table. I thought our ten-day retreats would continue many more years. That time is over. Other possibilities will arise. For a few days almost every week my husband Jack and I leave the city we love for the stone cottage of my dreams, a retreat in the woods with a murmuring brook that alters the rhythm of our lives. Molly has visited us there; she and I have laughed and talked over meals, and looked at pages together, pen in hand.

Via language we intimate, consciously or subliminally, the essence of who we are; yet much of who we are to others (and to ourselves) may seem incomprehensible, remain a mystery. *Do you read me?* That's what we ask, sometimes through static, hoping our words have travelled across a distance and arrived. Something essential has been said. Is the quality of the transmission sufficiently clear? With those same words we ask someone to affirm that the essence of what we mean, what we intend, is understood. What more could one ask—of a reader, a writer, a friend?

Phillis Levin
New York City and West Cornwall, Connecticut

ENDNOTES

1   "I Was a Girl, a Gray Queen," Molly Peacock transl., Greg Delanty and Michael Matto eds. *The Word Exchange: Anglo-Saxon Poems in Translation* (W. W. Norton and Company, 2011), 455.

2   The full quote from Whistler is: "Paint should not be applied thick…It should be like breath on the surface of a pane of glass." Marc Simpson, ed., *Like Breath on Glass: Whistler, Inness and the Art of Painting Softly* (Sterling and Francine Clark Art Institute, 2008), 3–4.

3   Howard Nemerov, "Storm Windows," *The Collected Poems of Howard Nemerov* (University of Chicago Press, 1981).

4   Phillis acquired the ring a few years later, though I visualize her wearing it then.

5   Peter Stitt, "Objective Subjectivities (*on Willingly* by Tess Gallagher; *Raw Heaven* by Molly Peacock; *The Evolution of the Flightless Bird* by Richard Kenney; T*he Sorrow of Architecture* by Liam Rector; *& A Wave* by John Ashbery)," (*The Georgia Review*, Fall, 1984), 631.

6   Molly Peacock, "Rhyme and the Line" from *A Broken Thing: Poets on the Line* eds. Emily Rosko and Anton Vander Zee (University of Iowa Press, 2011), 176–77.

7   Kay Ryan, "I Go to AWP," *Poetry Magazine*, October, 2005. www.poetryfoundation.org/poetrymagazine/articles/68318/i-go-to-awp "Molly Peacock is a late-add to the decimated panel, but she says a nice thing. She says it's wrong to think of the sonnet as a "container" or prison; instead, it is a "skeleton," which allows something to live and move. I can see a beautiful, animated X-ray of a galloping horse. This is a muscular and vigorous feeling about form."

8   Emily Dickinson, #540, Thomas Johnson, ed. *The Complete Poems of Emily Dickinson* (Boston, Little, Brown and Company, 1960), 263.

9   John Clare, "I Am," *Poems Chiefly from Manuscript*, Project Gutenberg-TM E-book 8672, August, 2005 location 2582.

10 Molly Peacock, Excerpts from "Self Portraits" in *How to Read a Poem*, (Riverhead, 1999 and McClelland and Stewart, 1999) 62–71.

11 Molly Peacock, Excerpts from "Introduction," *Poetry in Motion: 100 Poems from the Subways and Buses* (W. W. Norton and Company, 1996) 16–17.

12 Emily Dickinson, #372, R.W. Franklin, ed., *The Poems of Emily Dickinson* (Cambridge and London, The Belknap Press of Harvard University Press, 1999), 170.

13 Molly Peacock, Excerpts from "Preface," *In Fine Form*, Second Edition (Caitlin Press, 2016) 13–14.

14 Phillis Levin, "Introduction," *The Penguin Book of the Sonnet: 500 Years of a Classic Tradition in English* (Penguin Random House, 2001), xxxvii–xxxix.

15 Molly Peacock, Excerpts from "Prologue," *The Best Canadian Poetry in English*, (Tightrope Books, 2008) vii–x.

16 Charlotte Mew, "The Trees Are Down," Evan Boland, ed. Editor *Selected Poems* (Carcanet Press, 2008) 627-28.

17 Molly Peacock, Excerpts from "Charlotte Mew: The Trees Are Down," Joy Katz and Kevin Prufer, eds. *Dark Horses: Poets on Overlooked Poems* (University of Illinois Press, 2007) 116—118.

18 This is a variant on the favorite phrase attributed to Henry James, "summer afternoon."

The quote in the dedication is the first line of "Friends" by Molly Peacock in *Cornucopia: New and Selected Poems*.

ACKNOWLEDGMENTS

Grateful acknowledgement is made to the following publishers, and journals, and to their editors for permission to include texts of poems and excerpts from essays:

"Beets" and "Definition" from THE AFTERIMAGE by Phillis Levin, copyright © 1995 by Phillis Marna Levin. Used by permission of Copper Beech Press. All rights reserved.

"Table Manners" from MERCURY: POEMS by Phillis Levin, copyright © 2001 by Phillis Marna Levin. Used by permission of Penguin Books, an imprint of Penguin Publishing Group, a division of Penguin Random House LLC. All rights reserved.

Excerpt(s) from THE PENGUIN BOOK OF THE SONNET: 500 YEARS OF A CLASSIC TRADITION IN ENGLISH edited by by Phillis Levin, copyright © 2001 Phillis Marna Levin. Used by permission of Viking Books, an imprint of Penguin Publishing Group, a division of Penguin Random House LLC. All rights reserved.

"Box in Eden" and "To the Forest" from MAY DAY by Phillis Levin, copyright © 2008 by Phillis Marna Levin. Used by permission of Penguin Books, an imprint of Penguin Publishing Group, a division of Penguin Random House LLC. All rights reserved.

"Tabula Rasa" from MR. MEMORY & OTHER POEMS by Phillis Levin, copyright © 2016 by Phillis Marna Levin. Used by permission of Penguin Books, an imprint of Penguin Publishing Group, a division of Penguin Random House LLC. All rights reserved.

WITH THANKS

A Friend Sails in on a Poem came about through the suggestion of the flexible and gifted Jim Johnstone, Poetry Editor at Palimpsest Press and with the zesty guidance of the poet Jason Guriel, author of *Molly Peacock: A Critical Edition.* I owe them huge gratitude for guiding this project. My deep thanks go to publisher Aimee Parent Dunn as well as to the imaginative and hardworking production team: cover designer Ellie Hastings, copyeditor Ashley Van Elswyk, and social media manager Kristina Tiessen. As always, I am grateful to Emily McKibbon for her good judgement.

I owe supreme thanks to Phillis Levin, who allowed me to investigate our friendship, to comment on her poems and our process, and to reveal facts of our lives. Phillis saw every word of this book many times, and she graciously corrected many misconceptions I had as well as the various mistakes I managed to make about the facts of her life, all the while taking the time to write the Afterword that completes this book.

Thanks as well to publishers of my poems, W.W. Norton and Company, Biblioasis, McClelland and Stewart Penguin Random House, and the publishers of Phillis Levin's poems, University of Georgia Press, Copper Beech Press, and Penguin Random House. All have been generous in their permissions for reprints of our work.

A Friend Sails in on a Poem is the product of one poet's view of two poet's lives. It wouldn't have been written without my background as a biographer, and for that I thank the Leon Levy Center for Biography at The CUNY Graduate Center. I also want to mention the friends and writers who have influenced me over time, and whose thoughts or writing or conversations, sometimes from the distant past, have stayed with me, surfacing in these pages. Thank you: John Barton, Jill Bialosky, Lara Bozabalian, Stephanie Bolster, Lorna Crozier, James Cummins, Janice Eidus, Barbara Feldon, Michael Fried, Michael Fraser, Jonathan Galassi, Dana Gioia, Sue Goyette, Rachel Hadas, Helen Humphreys, Anita Lahey, Sonnet L'Abbe, Daniel Lawless, Jacob MacArthur Mooney, A.F. Moritz, Ricardo Maldonado, Walter Mosely, Marilyn Nelson, Jim Nason, Donna Bailey Nurse, Elise Paschen, Katha Pollitt, Ellen Rachlin, Dale Matthews Satorsky, Jason Schneiderman, Dan Simpson, Tom Sleigh, Carmine Starnino, Ricardo Sternberg, Fiona Sze-Lorraine, Halli Villegas, Heather Wood, and Lisa Zeidner.

MOLLY PEACOCK is the author of seven poetry collections, including *The Analyst: Poems*, *The Second Blush*, *Cornucopia: New and Selected Poems*, *Original Love*, *Take Heart*, *Raw Heaven* and *And Live Apart*. She is the author of *How to Read a Poem & Start a Poetry Circle*, co-editor of *Poetry in Motion: 100 Poems from the Subways and Buses*, and editor of *The Private I: Privacy in a Public World*. Peacock is also the author of a memoir, *Paradise, Piece by Piece*, two biographies about the lives of women visual artists: *The Paper Garden: Mrs. Delany Begins Her Life's Work at 72* and *Flower Diary: Mary Hiester Reid Paints, Travels, Marries & Opens a Door*, and a play, *The Shimmering Verge*. She founded *The Best Canadian Poetry* annual series. A former President of the Poetry Society of America, she co-founded *Poetry in Motion* on New York's subways and buses. Among her honors are Fellowships from the Canada Council for the Arts, National

Endowment for the Arts, Access Copyright, The Leon Levy Center for Biography, the Institute for Citizens and Scholars, the New York State Council on the Arts, the Ingram Merrill and the Danforth Foundations. Her poems have appeared in leading literary journals such as *Poetry, The Malahat Review, CV2, The Women's Review of Books, Liber, The Paris Review, The New Yorker, The Nation, Poetry London,* and *Plume* and are anthologized in *The Oxford Book of American Poetry* and *The Best American Poetry*. Her latest project is Molly Peacock's Secret Poetry Room at Binghamton University. The widow of James Joyce scholar Michael Groden, she is a dual citizen of Canada and the US and teaches for the Unterberg Poetry Center 92NY.

PHOTO © SIGRID ESTRADA

PHILLIS LEVIN is the author of five collections, most recently, *Mr. Memory & Other Poems* (Penguin Books, 2016), a finalist for the 2016 Los Angeles Times Book Prize. Her other volumes are *May Day* (Penguin Books, 2008), *Mercury* (Penguin Books, 2001), *The Afterimage* (Copper Beech Press, 1995), and *Temples and Fields* (University of Georgia Press, 1988). She is the editor of *The Penguin Book of the Sonnet* (Penguin USA, 2001; Allen Lane/The Penguin Press, 2001). Her honors include the Poetry Society of America's Norma Farber First Book Award, a Fulbright Scholar Award to Slovenia, the Amy Lowell Poetry Travelling Scholarship, and fellowships from the Ingram Merrill Foundation, the Guggenheim Foundation, the Bogliasco Foundation, and the National Endowment for the Arts. Her poems have appeared in *AGNI, The Atlantic, The Best American Poetry,*

Kenyon Review, The Nation, New Republic, The New Yorker, The New York Times Sunday Magazine, The Paris Review, Ploughshare, Plume, PN Review, Poetry, Poetry London, The Poetry Review (UK), *The Yale Review,* and other publications. A professor of English and poet-in-residence at Hofstra University, Levin lives with her husband in New York City and in West Cornwall, Connecticut. She has completed a sixth collection and is working on a memoir.